D0021236

WELCOME TO OBAMALAND

WELCOME TO OBAMALAND

I HAVE SEEN YOUR FUTURE AND IT DOESN'T WORK

JAMES DELINGPOLE

Since 1947
REGNERY
PUBLISHING, INC.
An Eagle Publishing Company • Washington, DC

Cataloging-in-Publication data on file with the Library of Congress

ISBN 978-1-59698-588-9

Published in the United States by
Regnery Publishing, Inc.
One Massachusetts Avenue, NW
Washington, DC 20001
www.regnery.com

Manufactured in the United States of America
10 9 8 7 6 5 4 3 2 1

Books are available in quantity for promotional or premium use. Write to Director of Special Sales, Regnery Publishing, Inc., One Massachusetts Avenue NW, Washington, DC 20001, for information on discounts and terms or call (202) 216-0600.

To my darling children: may your futures work!

CONTENTS

I Have Seen America's Future and It Doesn't Work

THINK OF ME AS THE HERO of H. G. Wells's *The Time Machine*, bursting into your present, my clothes all tattered and torn, and on my face an expression of dire horror and impending doom. For I am afraid I have a terrible message to impart. I have just seen the future. Your future. And I'm sorry to say it sucks.

This new president you've elected. You think he's going to make everything okay, right? Even if you didn't vote for him, you're kind of hoping that some good must surely come of it. He's young, he's personable, he's the same attractive shade as Tiger Woods, and he had nothing to do with the recession or the credit crunch or the mistakes that were made in Iraq or Afghanistan or any of the other old-regime bad things. This handsome JFK-revisited guy is going to magically sweep away all those bad things with his magic new broom. Right?

Ha ha ha ha ha.

Ha ha ha ha ha.

That's the sound of me laughing darkly, by the way.

You see, where you are now, so my country was twelve years ago when we elected our very own prototype of your shiny, grinning Obama guy.

The man's name was Blair, Tony Blair, someone to whom you're likely quite well disposed. From the American perspective I can see he must have seemed a pretty good thing. He stood shoulder to shoulder with your last president in the War on Terror. He understood the nature of the threat (as many still do not) and committed his fair share of fighting troops (unlike some pantywaist nations I could name, and will indeed name later). He wasn't afraid to be called Bush's poodle (which he certainly was over here, all too frequently).

But what you're less likely to know—and I don't blame you; why should you? If I lived in a country like yours that had everything, I doubt I'd worry about some two-bit, has-been island-state across the pond—is what a mess he made of his country. My country. The land I love at least as much as you love yours, (possibly more: wait till you read the fox-hunting chapter), and that I now fear is lost forever.

This would be my first warning to you: if you think your new president and his whomping Democratic majorities in both houses of Congress can't do any serious harm to your vast, resilient country, that their socialist bromides might not, in the end, mark "the end of the American idea" (to quote Mark Steyn)—well, you're quite wrong. Smiling socialists can do a great deal of damage indeed.

In 1997, when Tony Blair took over, Britain was still a pretty great place. Thanks to the economic reforms of Prime Minister Margaret Thatcher it had been transformed from the sick man of Europe—over-taxed, over-regulated, in thrall to the trade unions' dinosaurs—into a vibrant, confident power. We were happy; we had more money than we knew what to do with; we believed anything was possible. (Hence our reason for electing the charlatan who had promised us the earth.)

Twelve years on, we're so screwed we might as well be Burkina Faso. Our economy is in ruins. We're very afraid, and understandably so, for of all the G7 nations, our economy has officially been named the feeblest, the most out-of-control, and the one least likely to make a quick recovery from the global depression.

And it wasn't as though things were looking good even before the global economy went belly up. Blair's constitutional meddling replaced our venerable House of Lords with "Tony's Cronies," "devolved" regional parliaments on Wales and Scotland (so that even more taxpayer money could be wasted on government), and left our country more divided than at any time since the 1707 act of union; knife and gun crime was rocketing; fuel and food costs were soaring; our railroad system was collapsing; our roads were clogging; our filthy crowded hospitals were almost as likely to kill you as to cure you; our schools' standards were plummeting; our Mickey Mouse universities were becoming a joke; our traditional, hard-won freedoms as the world's oldest democracy were increasingly circumscribed by petty, micromanaging, nanny-ish laws governing every aspect of our behavior from the games our kids could play at school, to the kind of light bulbs we could use, to how often we could dispose of our trash, to the sort of jokes it was permissible to tell. We'd gone, in terrifyingly short space, from being a thriving capitalist state to a failed socialist experiment.

How did it all happen? How is it possible that the hard won liberties and revered traditions we spent over a millennium evolving were able to be trashed in just over a decade by a gang of political imbeciles? How were we ever so foolish as to give them so much power? How did we allow them to get away with doing so much damage for so long?

Well, you're about to find out: because I suspect it's about to happen to you.

In our case, New Labour lucked out by inheriting an economic boom—now gone bust—and so long as the mob had their bread and circuses, their iPods, their cheap flights to Ibiza, their Sat Navs, their widescreen TVs showing the Premiership (that's soccer) on Sky Sport, none of them much minded the fact their country was going to hell in a handcart, if they even noticed. If your idea of culture extends from David Beckham to *X Factor* by way of—at a push—the collected works of Dan Brown, you're hardly going to concern yourself overmuch about, say, the disappearance of Latin, grammar, hard science, rigor, or Shakespeare from the school curriculum. If you're a member of our burgeoning underclass, you're hardly likely to be troubled by the startling rise in crime, because you might be rather criminally minded yourself. If you're one of the endless categories of people convinced, thanks to the relentless inculcation of whinerdom that is part and parcel of the Left, that you're a victim of society's injustice, you're hardly like to complain about an ever more intrusive nanny state full of ever more expensive government programs that rob Peter to pay allegedly victimized Paul.

Far more culpable were the rich and better educated, most of my friends among them. These people, you might have hoped, would have employed their intelligence, their market savvy, their knowledge of history, to question some of the Blair regime's wilder claims for its own integrity and brilliance. Very few of them did. To criticize Blair in those early days was like being the boy in the fairy story who cried the emperor was wearing no clothes. This didn't make you popular with the crowd all around you, for they didn't want to be made to feel like dupes. In a world where, thanks to moral relativism (one of the Left's not-so-secret weapons), everyone believes whatever weird variant of reality they want to believe, no one is going to thank you for speaking the truth.

To be a right-wing libertarian in those early days was to feel rather as many of you reading this book must feel now. You know you're right, damn it. Your political philosophy is the most honest (it's about how the world is rather than how it ought to be), the most pragmatic, the one most effectively proven by precedent, and the one best guaranteed to make the world a better place for everyone. Problem is, it just doesn't fit in with the prevailing fashion. And in politics, unfortunately, fashion counts for rather more than integrity or ideology.

You've seen this in spades (excuse the expression) with Barack Obama, whom some of us think is far more style than substance, a man of self-serving gestures rather than selfless genius, of soaring speeches rather than serious statesmanship, of sneaking socialism (which is what you're about to get) rather than economic sobriety, and a man your press has crowned with a laurel wreath. In reverse of the Roman tradition, your press has trotted behind Obama's conquering chariot, whispering in his ear, "You are a god." And they've done an excellent job of defending his presumed divinity. During his election campaign, Obama seemed invulnerable to embarrassments that would have sunk lesser candidates—from the crazed rantings of a racist preacher (whom Obama said had been "like family" to him) as he damned America and theorized that AIDS was invented by the American government to kill black people, to Obama's connections to an unrepentant domestic terrorist, to the sainted one's rise in the not so very holy Democrat-machine politics of Chicago.

In Britain, we'd seen this before with Tony Blair, another smiling candidate, speaking a new language, who convinced us all—or far too many of us—that he wasn't a dangerous socialist, not like the ones we'd kept out of power by electing Margaret Thatcher and John Major.

The popularity ratings Blair enjoyed at his peak were the highest of any post-war prime minister—higher than Thatcher, higher than Winston Churchill. Nothing could touch him: not claims that he had taken party political donations for business favors, not his grotesque mishandling of a serious Foot and Mouth outbreak, not the lamentable folly of the Millennium Dome, not the venality and incompetence of his ministers, not his chancellor Gordon Brown's growing taxes, not his baffling failure to achieve a single one of his targets on welfare reform, hospital waiting lists (yeah that's right: and you wonder why Britain comes so low in international cancer survival rate league tables?), or child literacy. Blair was bulletproof. His government was bulletproof. If it promised it was going to do something then the electorate believed it, not withstanding an increasingly long list of promises unfulfilled. No British government had ever lied to and cheated its people in quite this systematic way before (at least not since the openly corrupt days of the eighteenth and early nineteenth century). So the government had a good 150 years of public faith in the integrity of the parliamentary system to exploit. And exploit it, it most shamelessly did.

Now that pretty much the whole country has woken up from that twelve-year party with a screaming hangover, noticed that their pockets are empty, their savings gone, their property trashed to virtual worthlessness, their streets rife with crime, their liberties circumscribed by nannying bureaucrats, people have started to wonder: "Huh? Did someone drug me? Why didn't I see that one coming?"

As one who did see it coming, I find it hard to summon much sympathy. It's like Dr. Faustus complaining when, having been granted the power to enjoy his every earthly fantasy, the devil turns up at the end to steal away his soul. It's like the citizens of Hamlyn complaining when, having welshed on their deal with the Pied Piper, he lures all their children inside the mountain. You just want to give these guys a good shake—maybe a brisk slap on the cheeks for good measure—and say: "Did you think it was going to come

FREE, this once-in-a-lifetime wonder deal you made with the mysterious, dark stranger you met at the crossroads at midnight?"

The bad news is that you're about to go through the same experience. Obama's administration is going to persuade most Americans, as Blair's administration persuaded most Britons, that the impossible is true: that big government and efficient capitalism can work hand in hand, that state meddling in your life will not make you any less free, that government knows better how to spend your money than you do, that socialism isn't a dirty word but a good and noble idea that has been misapplied and misrepresented and is now ripe for another try, only we're going to do it properly this time.

So what, if any, consolation do I have to offer you in these dark and difficult times? Precious little, I'm afraid. Virtually nothing in fact, save the warm, self-affirmatory glow you get when someone tells you you're right, that some day your beliefs will be vindicated, that however long it takes, reality will win out.

It isn't easy being right when pretty much everyone else is wrong. I know. I wrote a whole book about it. It was called *How to Be Right* and it catalogued in shocked, despairing detail all those superficially well-meaning but utterly wrongheaded left-liberal schemes that were supposed to make our world a better place but have made it so much worse. I talked about *foie gras* ("If God really cared so much about animal rights, why would He have made *foie gras* taste so delicious"), about the lie of passive smoking, about the wussiness of the Germans (once the terror of the free world, now such Eurowimps they won't even let their Luftwaffe fly at night in Afghanistan because of health und safety regulations), about the much overrated plight of polar bears, about Rachel "Silent Spring" Carson's unacknowledged role as one of the twentieth century's great mass murderers.

Did it make me feel better when I'd got it all off my chest? Not much. When I finished the book the world still sucked as much as ever it did when I started. In fact, being as the liberal lefties were still in charge, it had got even worse. But what did buoy me quite a bit were the large numbers of people who wrote and e-mailed me to say what a chord I'd struck. They'd been beginning to think that they were the only sane people left in the world. Yet here, they were delighted to discover, was somebody else who thought as they did. Someone who didn't buy all the fashionable cant. Someone who still believed, above all, in liberty.

In this book, I hope to provide a similar service for all you right-thinking Americans. I offer it as an act of homage to a great country and a great people I love nearly as much my own. There's not a lot you can do to stop the deluge of misery which is going to hit you now that the socialists are in charge. But forewarned is forearmed. The more of you who know what to expect of social-ism, the more of you will be ready to resist and restrain its wilder excesses.

Chapter One

NEVER TRUST A HIPPIE

HOW DID THE NICE GUYS—you know, like sweet, gentle, progressive Obama, fresh from the effete finishing school of Chicago machine politics—get to be so nasty? That's the question some of you are going to be asking over the coming weeks, months, years, eons.

Not all of you, I know. To some of you it will come as no surprise whatsoever that a left-liberal president and a Congress run by the likes of Harry Reid and Nancy Pelosi can do so many stupid, wrongheaded, unfair, and often downright mean, bullying, and destructive things. But you'd be amazed how many of your friends will have been expecting, or at least hoping, for something better than that.

It was just the same in Britain when young, grinning, snappy-suited Tony Blair came into power on a bright sunny day in June 1997. Here was the birth of a glorious new dawn, everyone said.

There was a new sheriff in town, and not only did he have nice gleaming teeth, great personal charm, and a plausible manner, he also had ideas: ideas of how to bridge the divide between rich and poor; how to erase the injustices of the past and build a new Jerusalem; how to make a Britain fit for the many, not just the few; how to bring about greater equality but—and here was the cunning part, the one no politician had ever had the gall to promise before—without jeopardizing the nation's prosperity.

"Excellence for all," was Blair's stated aim. And in that nonsensical phrase—which sounds rather Obamaesque, doesn't it?—was encapsulated the essential intellectual bankruptcy of the whole Blair project.

"Look, it's just not possible for everyone and everything to be excellent," some of us wanted to protest. "If you have winners there are going to be losers. In order for something to be excellent something else has to be less than excellent. Otherwise the very concept of excellence is utterly meaningless."

But in those early days, the cheering onlookers in the crowd didn't want to listen to the boy who was shouting, "But the Emperor's wearing no clothes." They saw what they wanted to see. And what they saw made them very happy indeed. At last they had the kind of leader who talked their language. Not some handbag-wielding tyrant like Margaret Thatcher; not some bumbler like John Major; but a guy who was going to absolve them of social guilt *and* make them richer. Blair called it "The Third Way."

Now some of us, as I say, could tell straight away that Blair was nothing more than a snake-oil salesman.

As with the "excellence for all," so with the "Third Way": it's a non-starter, an impossible concept. You can have either more of the Left way or more of the Right way. There's no clever third option no one thought of before.

Take the key issue of taxation. I'm no economist, but if there's one basic fact I do know it's that the more you tax people the less they have to spend; the less they spend, the more slowly—if at all—the economy grows. So if you want everyone to get richer, tax them less. And if you want everyone to get poorer—or at least, less rich—tax them more. Sure you can find middle ground between those two positions, but it doesn't transport you to some hitherto uncharted and wondrous territory where the paradigm changes. All that it means is that you're compromising.

Besides buying far too unquestioningly into his impossible message, another mistake people made in the early days of Tony Blair was to confuse personality with politics. "I'm a pretty straight kind of guy," Blair once famously said. (About an incident in which, ten years after the event, he was finally revealed to have been lying his pants off.) The idea—a kind of Western liberal version of the Kim Jong-il personality cult—was that if you liked the man (and you did: he had that chameleon charm, with an accent and manner that mutated to suit his every audience be they Welsh hill farmers, Geordie builders, or City bankers) you couldn't help but support his policies too.

It's true of Barack Obama. (And my, how it was true of Bill Clinton!) If you ever had the guy round to dinner, no matter how much you disagreed with his politics, he'd switch on his full-beam charm and you'd be going: "Wow! I love you, man! You're the greatest president in the history of the U. S. of A.!" No, sorry. You would.

Most politicians possess this capability to a certain degree. It's how they got to be elected. George W. Bush has it too, my friend the historian Andrew Roberts tells me. Of course, Andrew is a bit biased because Dubya happened to name his *A History of the English Speaking Peoples Since 1900* one of his favorite books ever, and went on to invite him to three dinners at the White House, once in the private dining room. Even so, when Roberts tells me that George W. Bush is "one of us. Incredibly bright and sharp. Just the funniest guy. Someone you'd definitely love to have to dinner—apart from the awkward problem that he doesn't drink," I can perfectly well believe him. You don't—usually—get to be leader of the free world by being a colorless drone.

So Barack Obama's a nice, plausible, personable guy. So what? First, as we've just agreed, it's his job to be that way. Second, it's not just Obama who's going to be running your country, is it? It's the whole left-liberal political machine. A machine run by people who aren't nearly as nice as President Obama. Who don't want to be and don't need to be. Guys like one Rahm Emanuel, Obama's very first appointment, the White House chief of staff, a political operator who makes even hardened Democrat political operatives turn pale and clammy with fear. It's the Emanuels you really want to be watching out for because they're the ones—not Obama: he's just a figurehead—who are going to be doing the most to ruin your life.

For most of his regime, Tony Blair had a hatchet man called Alastair Campbell to do his dirty work for him: Mister Nasty to Blair's Mister Nice. Campbell was a mouthy, ex-tabloid journalist who'd become Blair's secretary, hovering perpetually at his shoulder like some evil demon from a Philip Pullman novel, menacing anyone who tried to get too close, taking diligent notes (for his future lucrative diary), swearing like a trooper and ringing up TV producers and newspaper editors at all hours to abuse them whenever they ran a story he felt was insufficiently flattering to the Dear Leader.

There were others, equally villainous, in the Prime Minister's rogues' gallery.

- A jowly bruiser named Prescott—think Lurch without the charm—perpetually simmering with class hatred because he'd once had to work as a steward on a cruise liner, promoted far above his talents (to Deputy Prime Minister, no less) by a prime minister desperate to placate those left-wingers in his party who feared he was selling out to the bourgeoisie

- A serpentine charmer and Machiavellian fixer named Mandelson—now Lord Mandelson—known to all as the Prince of Darkness thanks to his uncanny ability to perpetrate the most wicked political deeds and make the most spectacular errors of judgement, yet still come out on top smelling of roses
- An extreme left-wing salamander-fancier named Livingstone, the controversial mayor of London, who considered it one of his primary functions to wage Marxist war against the bourgeoisie by cozying up to dictators like Hugo Chavez, courting Islamist hate-preachers such as Yusuf al-Qaradawi (a supporter of female genital mutilation, the execution of homosexuals, the destruction of the Jewish people, and the use of suicide bombs against civilians), squandering taxpayers' money on minority-interest events such as anti-racism festivals and gay pride marches, and employing at great expense his Marxist cronies, eight of whom received payoffs totalling $2 million following his defeat by the conservative candidate, Boris Johnson, in the London mayoral elections

I could go on but it's too depressing. I cite them merely to give you a taste of the smorgasbord of scuzzballs, incompetents, time-servers, Communists, class warriors, eco-loons, single-issue rabble-rousers, malcontents, and losers who always rise to the surface during a left-liberal administration.

You've seen some of these types in action before. The John Murthas and the Chuck Schumers. The James Carvilles and the Al Sharptons. The Barney Franks and the Henry Waxmans. And it's bearable when there's not too many of them. Almost amusing even because they can act as bogeymen: the whacko villains you just love to hate.

Where it becomes a problem—as you're about to discover, if you haven't already—is when your ruling administration consists of nothing but these people. No longer do they qualify as light relief. They become your daily nightmare.

What I want to do in this chapter is to explore in a little more detail that question I asked at the beginning, about how it is that the nice guys got to turn nasty. It will go a long way towards explaining, I think, how a government which comes into power on a ticket of giving your world a kinder, gentler, friendlier face can end up achieving the exact opposite.

By "nice" I'm referring to this image a lot of left-liberal people have of themselves—and which sometimes even us right-wingers are seduced into believing in—as the good guys, the ones who care, the ones who feel, the ones who are going to heal our broken society.

I'm going to do this by talking a little about my own political journey and by dragging you—screaming and kicking, I'd imagine, because it stinks and it's full of tofu-munching, tree-hugging, Obama-worshipping surrender monkeys, but I love it all the same—to Glastonbury Festival.

Glastonbury is how Woodstock would have been if it had been any good. Yeah, yeah, Joni Mitchell, Jimi Hendrix, Crosby, Stills, Nash, and Young, flowers in hair, epochal moment in the Age of Aquarius, blah blah blah. None of this alters the fact that Woodstock was a toilet which no one who was there really enjoyed because it was overcrowded, unsanitary, pissing down with rain, you couldn't get anywhere near close enough to see or hear the acts, and anyway everyone was bumming out on bad acid.

Glastonbury, it must be conceded, is not totally dissimilar. It happens in June every year on a dairy farm in Somerset sitting atop a natural clay bowl which means every time it rains—as it does every other year—the scene is transformed in moments from a lush, verdant, pastoral idyll into the Battle of Passchendaele (which, you'll surely know, is the one where men actually drowned in craters of liquid mud).

When it's sunny though, it's a gas. Because it has been going since 1971, it's had plenty of time to iron out most of the glitches that made Woodstock a bummer. Sure the toilets are still evil— (one memorable year, the shit-sucker machine that gets pulled along by a tractor and sucks all the shit out of the latrines into a huge tank accidentally went on to "blow" when it should have been on "suck" and turned two dozen or so very unhappy festival goers brown)—sure the middle of a close-packed crowd of 20,000 is not the ideal place to get a sudden attack of drugs paranoia, sure a lot of it resembles Barter Town from *Mad Max II*. But for us regulars, this is all part of its quaint charm. Like the surf scene in *Apocalypse Now*, it's hell—but *fun* hell.

I've been going non-stop since 1990 and in that time I've seen pretty much every band or musician that's worth seeing: Radiohead; Johnny Cash; Paul McCartney (not his fault he's a freaking veggie—no wait, it is); The Killers; Underworld; P. J. Harvey. One particularly memorable moment was when the great, high Sixties psychedelic band Love reformed and, as the sun went down, played the whole of their 1967 masterpiece *Forever Changes*. Normally when aging bands play their old stuff, they turn it into some sort of perfunctory greatest hits medley because they've done it too often before and they're bored. Not Love. Because their crazed lead singer Arthur Lee had spent most of the intervening period in prison on firearms offenses, he was playing it as if for the first time: straight off the record, echt hippy psychedelia preserved in aspic, mariachi brass and all. It was sublime.

Even better than the music at Glastonbury is the "vibe." Some say it has to do with the confluence of so many Ley lines on the site; or perhaps with the rumoured presence nearby—book your flight now, Dan Brown junkies—of the Holy Grail which Joseph of Arimathea brought to Glastonbury Abbey. Others say that this is what happens when you get 100,000 nice, middle-class kids in a field together, 99,999 of them on pot, mushrooms, or Ecstasy. Either way it's mellow and easygoing and abundant with the spirit of peace and love.

You'll sit down on one of the makeshift benches by the campfire in the Tiny Tea Tent with your mug of chai, and instantly strike up a conversation with your neighbor, knowing that at Glastonbury there's no such thing as a stranger, only a friend you've never met. Someone will start playing the didgeridoo. Another will be pounding out a rhythm on his Djembe drum. A fat joint will be passed round. A homely middle-aged woman with a bindi in the middle of her forehead will voluntarily begin manipulating your chakras. "Wow!" you start thinking. "We could build ourselves a whole new civilization here. One run by organic food collectives, tai chi sifus, earth mothers, zero balancers, and bearded old men called Dragonsbane who parade in white flowing robes round Stonehenge every year for the Winter Solstice!"

Then the drugs wear off, reality kicks in, it's back to the day job and that's it for another year. And where's the harm in any of that?

That's what I always used to think in the early days at any rate, before the truth dawned. I couldn't tell you exactly what year I had my blinding revelation. Probably it didn't happen in one go but by installments.

But there's one particular episode I do remember quite vividly. Elbow—moody, sensitive Manchester band; lovely tunes: you'd like 'em, apart from the politics; but then if you judged bands on their politics you could never play another record—were playing on the main stage and encouraging all of us in the crowd to sing-a-long to one of their choruses.

The lyrics went: "We still believe in love. So, fuck you."

This was the time of the Second Gulf War, so it was obvious to everyone who the words were aimed at. Here was the defiant message of the people of Britain—well, the kids of Glastonbury—to the evil, dumb, hateful George Bush and his poodle Tony Blair.

"You two warmongers might enjoy bombing the hell out of innocent Iraqi orphans for the pure sadistic pleasure of it," the subtext of those lyrics ran. "But we, the caring people, the nice people, the good people think it's better to love than to hate."

Now I've never much liked audience sing-a-longs at the best of times. I can't sing, I always embarrass myself by not knowing the lyrics, and I don't much like having compulsory group activities imposed on me when I'm trying to relax and enjoy music performed by professionals rather than some amateur chorus of tuneless, brainless caterwaulers. But this was something else altogether.

As the singer Guy Garvey pointed his mic towards us for the second time—"We still be-lieve in lo-o-ve. So fuck you!"—I just couldn't go through with it.

I thought: "This is wrong! This is so wrong! I support the War on Terror. I think we're doing the right thing by invading Iraq to depose a guy who poison-gases Kurds, machine-guns Marsh Arabs, and feeds his Shia opposition into mincing machines! Why should I let this guy bully me into voicing an opinion I don't hold?"

The more I thought about it, the angrier I felt. It was the presumptuous arrogance of it I found so galling. (All the more so because in almost every respect Garvey is such a lovely, gentle, humble fellow.) The assumption was that anyone capable of appreciating good rock music, enjoying the occasional jazz cigarette, and drinking in the glorious Somerset air, must—as night follows day—hold the full standard set of left-liberal values, up to and including opposition to George W. Bush and the Iraq war.

And I just didn't.

It was from this point onwards that things that hadn't previously annoyed me about Glastonbury started to irk me very much indeed. Like the endless propaganda adverts for Greenpeace, broadcast on huge screens between sets, tacitly inviting us all to applaud their leftist agitators as they scaled the cooling towers of power stations and unfurled banners and generally made it harder for our electricity suppliers to get on with their healthy, decent business of powering our factories and lighting our homes. And the ones—this was more than I could bear—advertising Michael Moore's latest exercise in mendacious polemic *Fahrenheit 9/11*.

A man next to me—white, educated, well-paid: the kind of guy whose comfortable lifestyle owes everything to the value system Moore opposes—started applauding one of Moore's jokes.

"You think that treacherous, manipulative, fake ordinary Joe multi-millionaire is funny, do you?" I began muttering under my breath. "You think it was clever, do you, the line he came up with about if the passengers had all been black on those 9/11 planes, the Twin Towers would still be standing, because black guys don't take no shit, whereas stupid white men...."

And my wife had to drag me off, before we got in to a fight. (Very un-Glastonbury, that would have been.)

She dragged me to a food stall, often the best solution when I'm angry, but this time it only made things worse. You see, as I stood in the queue for my organic mung bean and tofu burger (or whatever), someone handed me a leaflet. It was from some campaigning body or other demanding the right for taxpayers to be able to opt out on having any of their money spent on defense.

Unfortunately, before I could take a swing at the guy he'd gone.

So I had to stand there brooding, going over and over again in my mind just what an utterly stupid and impractical and irresponsible and childish and pathetic idea this scheme was.

Would it mean then, I thought of asking any passing socialist, that childless couples should have the right not to have any of their tax money diverted into education or pediatric care? And that snobs who hate the poor should have the right to insist that none of their money goes towards welfare? And that people with private medical insurance should in no wise have any of their tax dollars wasted on Medicaid? And racists given the chance to segregate their money from black people?

And what if our country were ever invaded? What should be done about all the people who'd refused to allow their tax money to be spent on defense? Should they be sacrificed to the enemy in the first assault perhaps? Or made to do penance by walking across minefields in human waves, as the Chinese did during the Korean War? And what, alternatively, if our army was sent on some kind of humanitarian operation, perhaps distributing food to starving refugees? Ought they perhaps to distribute leaflets at the same time noting: "We wish to advise the people of this region that the following taxpayers dissociate themselves from this aid program: 'Aadvark, Andrew; Abrahams, Bob; Adams, Gerry. . . . '"

Here are few of the organizations and charitable causes you most likely won't find represented in the stalls at Glastonbury festival: the Countryside Alliance (which campaigns on behalf of field sports including shooting, fishing, and fox-hunting); the Taxpayers Alliance (which publicizes the amount of tax money squandered on idiot causes); charities for disabled servicemen; organizations promoting meat; organizations campaigning for the right of dedicated medical researchers not to have their homes fire-bombed and their families threatened by animal rights fanatics.

In the early days when I went to Glastonbury festival, none of this bothered me. I used to think it was quite fun playing at being a weekend hippie. I never used to mind that part of my ticket money went to Greenpeace and the Campaign for Nuclear Disarmament, nor that the only newspaper you could buy on site was the Left-wing Guardian, nor that almost every other stall seemed to be run by PETA or the Vegetarian Society or Drop the Debt (to cancel Third World debt). Maybe it didn't bother me because when I first started going to Glastonbury a conservative government was in charge, and it seemed only right and fair—and kind

of charming in its retro, let's-all-live-like-medieval-peasants way—
to see an alternative lifestyle being promoted in contrast to the
reigning hegemony.

But the moment a left-wing government comes into power, the
counterculture suddenly becomes the mainstream. And that's
when your problems begin. In opposition, the alternative lifestyle
may seem innocuous enough. When it becomes the dominant culture, however, it soon shows its true colors. Its colors are the
blood red of socialist revolutionaries everywhere: the colors of
intolerance and tyranny.

Q. How did the nice guys suddenly get to be so nasty?

A. They didn't. They were always that way. You just weren't
looking closely enough.

By nasty, I don't of course mean irrelevancies like character or
amount donated annually to charity or depth of rapport with
fluffy kittens. Personality oughtn't to come into this debate: that's
a left-wing hang-up. What I'm talking about is the ideology itself.

This isn't at all how the Left sees itself, as we know. It presents
itself as the nice ideology, the caring ideology, that altruistic ideology. But at its core is not a love of humanity but a visceral
hatred of it.

The left believes that man's nature—correction: "[Wo-]man's"
nature—is so irredeemably vile that he cannot be trusted on his
own to do the right thing. Left to his own devices, the Left
believes, man will instinctively tend towards vices like greed, selfishness, corruption, prejudice, jealousy, aggression, and competitiveness which inevitably result in a society riddled with injustice.
The best way to alleviate this injustice, therefore, is to constrain
the freedom of the individual to do as he pleases and correct his
behavior through the wise governance of the state. As a British
Labour politician famously put it in his 1937 book *The Case for
Socialism,* "The gentleman in Whitehall [the Civil Service, respon-

sible for enforcing governmental diktat] really does know better what is good for people than the people know themselves."

Conservatives willingly grant that man has his darker side—why else do we have wars, torture, *American Idol?*—but we also know that, left to his own devices, man tends towards good not ill. He forms natural bonds—family, friends, communities of interest, business partnerships, religious ties—which create social cohesion and harmony far more effective than any government can engender. And even his supposedly "bad" qualities often lead to useful ends. Greed, for example, is what causes men to take the risks that stimulate economic growth and (well, usually) make society richer. Therefore conservatives believe—though more on an instinctive level: it's not the sort of thing we would usually voice because it sounds so touchy-feely—human nature is something to be cherished. We believe, above all, in the quality that gives human nature its best hope of self expression: liberty.

So whereas the Left likes to think of itself as progressive, fair, and kindly, its deeper instincts are pessimism, misanthropy, bullying, and control. To understand this is to understand almost everything you need to know about the Left: why there's such a gulf between the lofty heights of its stated aims and the stygian depths of misery caused by its policies; why it will always seek to extend its grip over the individual and the family (whose independence it sees as an affront to decency); why it is unerringly drawn to those causes most inimical to the greater interests of humanity—such as animal rights and the current green movement.

It has become a commonplace on the political right that "green is the new red." But the reason it's a cliché is because it's true. With the fall of the Berlin Wall and the collapse of Communism—brought about, of course, by the humor and cool-headed brinkmanship of a great, right-wing president, Ronald Reagan—the ideologues of the Far Left found themselves in sudden, dire need of a new cause. It needed to be one which, like Communism, combined high-mindedness, control-freakery, and austerity with a burning hatred of the capitalist system. The international green movement fitted in with that need just perfectly.

Later, I shall be discussing in more detail how it is that a movement born with the noblest of aims—to preserve nature and the glories of the world for the benefit of all mankind—should since have been so corrupted that it poses an active and real threat to our well-being and our economic future. But hey, isn't that the Left all over: good intentions paving the highway to hell.

For now I'll give you just one example. It concerns Rachel Carson, author of the landmark 1962 bestseller *Silent Spring*. Ask any environmentalist of a certain age what it was that set them on the path to enlightenment and this is the book they cite. Everyone read it and almost everyone believed its apocalyptic predictions of a cancer epidemic that could hit "practically one hundred percent" of the human population and of birdlife being wiped out— all because of man's use of the deadly insecticide DDT.

The hysteria generated by Carson's "classic" led to the ban on DDT which deprived the developing world of its most cost-effective control against mosquitoes and, by extension, the millions of extra needless deaths caused by malaria. So it is that the poster girl of the modern green movement could plausibly be accused of being one of the twentieth century's greatest mass murderers.

And maybe, if there had been a scintilla of truth in Carson's claims, she'd have more of a moral get out. Problem is, pretty much everything she says in the book is nonsense. DDT doesn't give you cancer. It doesn't, *pace Silent Spring*, damage bird reproduction. Carson's brand of junk science and misanthropic anti-capitalist doom-mongering has provided the model for the greens ever since.

This is what I finally appreciated about that time in Glastonbury: that far from being just another fluffy lifestyle choice which shows you're one of the good guys, the ideology of the Left is a truly malign and dangerous thing. And what makes it all the more dangerous is precisely this shiny, loveable image it has somehow managed to secure itself, while simultaneously managing to tar anyone to the right of them as belonging to the dark side.

Part of the Left's huge popular appeal, I'm sure, is that it requires no deep thought, no analysis. Vote Blair, vote Obama and your work is done: you have said all that needs to be said about the kind of person you are. Nice. Well-meaning. One of the gang. However, vote McCain, vote Bush, vote for anyone on the right and you automatically place yourself in a position where you are expected to justify yourself. "Look, you may think I did it because I'm a selfish bastard. But.... " It's one of the things that goes with the territory of being on the right. We're always having to fight our corner.

I suppose the upside of this is that we become unusually proficient at arguing and we develop a much better understanding than our equivalents on the Left of who we are and what we truly believe in. The downside is that it can become so terribly exhausting. Sure a juicy ding-dong row is fun once in a while. But every day? "This is James. Please don't be too offended by anything he says. See, the thing is, he's quite disgustingly right-wing...." And there you are stuck like some performing bear, expected to roar and snarl and lash out in your scary right-wing way for the delectation of your lefty bear-baiters.

Even more wearing than this right-wing entertainment act is the knowledge that you're so widely hated. Perhaps the greatest of all the victories the Left has won itself is to have persuaded the world that to be right-wing is not so much a political affiliation as proof of moral deficiency. We right-wingers aren't just misguided: we're repellent and evil. And again, it's fun being the boogeyman once in a while. I've always liked scaring the bejaysus out of old ladies and small children. But I do fear that this caricaturing of our

position tends unfairly to denigrate the high moral and intellectual seriousness in which we've adopted it.

God knows none of us chose to be conservative for the easy
ride, did we? It's hard being a conservative, much harder than
being a lefty. In fact I sometimes think it's akin to being like Neo
in *The Matrix*—only with all the cool stuff taken away from you.
You don't get the instant martial arts skills or the ability to run
through walls, catch bullets, or defeat exponentially growing
bands of enemies. But you do get the equivalent of that moment
in the movie where you have to decide which pill to take.

You know the scene I mean? Neo (Keanu Reeves) is given a
choice. If he takes one pill he can go to the safe, ordered, cozy,
familiar world he knew before, where all his friends are and he
can tuck into nice juicy steaks and never be aware that this world
is in fact just the sinister machines' construct. If he takes the other,
it's goodbye to that security forever: instead of steaks, mates, and
sunny L.A., only powdered rations, grey industriascapes, and the
constant threat of violent death.

That was the choice I had to make that time at Glastonbury.
The choice we conservatives have all had to make: between seeing the world as it is or the world as we'd like it to be; between
the spray-on niceness and ease of the glib, leftist consensus or the
opprobrium and rigor of conservatism.

I chose. It's why I'm writing this book.

Chapter Two

OUR ENEMY, THE STATE

MIND YOU, I'M A CONSERVATIVE, a proper family man burdened with responsibilities, trying desperately to earn enough money—such money as our socialist government won't rip from my pay check—to send my children to decent schools. But all the same, the mind wanders.

For instance, does it ever bother you that you have not had nearly enough random, meaningless sex with beautiful strangers? It bothers me, greatly, most of the time.

And this isn't a public plea for mercy sex by the way. If you saw how beautiful my wife is, you wouldn't feel sorry for me. And the very last thing I want is thousands upon thousands of gorgeous American females suddenly hurling themselves at me out of pity or kindness. I'm very happily married and intend to stay that way, an Anglican who even turns up at church occasionally, and I know that real sex is the kind that leads to children, of which I have three. Extra-marital sex—even extra-marital oral sex which I understand from one of your former presidents doesn't count as sex at all—is one of the many things that wives just won't understand.

No, I'm bothered more about it in that semi-regretful, semi-nostalgic way where you look back on your earlier life and try to figure out the mistakes you made and why they happened. Not getting enough sex was definitely one of them.

Now the thing that puzzles me, looking back at photos of me in that era, is how anyone could not have wanted to have sex with me. I don't think I'm being unduly immodest here. I wasn't a hunk. I most surely wasn't a love god. But I was cute. A bit buck-teethed maybe—but in England, as you may have noticed, we're much less squeamish than you are about that kind of detail. A bit on the short side (I'm 5 foot, 8 inches). A bit on the bad hair side (but this was the 1980s, so the problem was not mine alone). Definitely, though, a guy good-looking enough to make any prospective sexual partner think: "You know what? It wouldn't be the worst ordeal imaginable."

Or so you would have thought they would have thought. But they didn't. Well, a few of them did, but not nearly as many as I would have liked. And the question I've been asking myself ever since is "Why?" Only in a rhetorical way, though, because the answer is obvious and I've known it for a very long time.

It is all the fault of the Left.

In fact almost everything that's wrong with the world is the fault of the Left, as I hope fully to demonstrate in the course of this book.

By left I, of course, mean the political left. For variety's sake I shan't always call it that. Sometimes I shall say liberals, or left-liberals, or lefties. Sometimes I shall extend it to include Eco Fascists, Hippies, and Greens. Sometimes I shall blame Socialism, the State, the Nanny State, Big Government, or if I'm trying to be clever and sound like the Political Studies graduate I'm not (in fact I majored in English literature), collectivism or even Marxism. As far as I'm concerned it all amounts to the same thing and that thing is: Bad.

Yes I'm dimly aware that strictly speaking these terms aren't interchangeable. But on this matter, I feel rather as the great Samuel Johnson did when asked who was worse—Voltaire or Rousseau. The good doctor replied: "Sir, there is no settling the point of precedency between a louse and a flea." And Dr. Johnson, as you surely know, was right about most things. Not least when asked to identify the first Whig (the first liberal). "The first Whig was the Devil!" he said.

This book, you'll gather, is not the sort to let itself get bogged down in too much tedious technical detail. There's plenty of enough of that already in any number of American tomes, from the classic and intellectual, like Russell Kirk's *The Conservative Mind*, to the more tub-thumping contemporary, like Newt Gingrich's *Real Change*. What interests me far more are the practical day-to-day things that really matter—family, friends, good food, hunting, a decent game of bridge, a bigger home, a better life, and above all liberty—for it is from liberty that everything that makes life worthwhile springs.

When I use all those various Left euphemisms, what I'm getting at basically is one single poisonous idea: that the State knows better than you do how you should live your life.

It doesn't. If you take only one idea from this book make it that one. Repeat after me: "I know what's best for me, not the State. I know best how to spend my money, NOT the State."

Of course you know this. If you didn't know it you wouldn't have bought this book. You'd be reading some piece of toss by Al Gore, or Noam Chomsky, or Michael Moore.

But the reason you need to keep reminding yourself what you already know is that over the coming months and years there will be so many weasely attempts to persuade you otherwise. You'll be told that people who think the way you do are selfish, misguided, nasty, impractical, and wedded to an old ideology that has now been discredited. You'll be told that there's another way—what our Prime Minister Blair called a Third Way—in which government and individuals can work hand in hand to make the world a better, fairer, happier place.

Don't you believe it, though many will. You're about to experience the *Invasion of the Bodysnatchers* effect. No longer will you know which of your friends you can trust and which have gone over the dark side. Remember what happened to that nice Donald Sutherland at the end? Well Christopher Buckley is his Obama-world equivalent. If they can get to him, they can get to anyone.

Anyway, more of that later. I was telling you about why it was that my failure to get enough sex in the Eighties—most of the Nineties too, come to think about it—was all the Left's fault. I blame the Left on at least two levels for this: the macro one and the micro one.

First, the micro one. In the Eighties, you'll remember, a terrible new scourge appeared among us. AIDS was its name and it was going to kill us all. In case any of us would-be sexual adventurers failed to get the message, our government drove its message home with a series of hard-hitting TV commercials. One showed the letters A I D S being hewn out of grim, grey rock to form the shape of a gravestone. "AIDS!" went the gravelly, deep, funereal, voiceover. "DON'T DIE OF IGNORANCE."

Little did we know it at the time but ignorance was exactly what our government was promoting. The state's official line was that AIDS was an equal opportunities disease, which liked to kill you irrespective of race, color, creed, sexual preference, or practice of sharing needles when shooting up heroin. Yet as the most cursory statistical evidence would have shown, even in those early days, AIDS incidence was confined almost totally to certain discrete and readily identifiable groups.

Number one target for the disease were homosexual men, especially those with multiple partners, and even more especially those who practised unprotected anal sexual intercourse. Next on the list were haemophiliacs who'd contracted the disease through contaminated blood. People of African origin seemed especially prone to it too. So were people who shared needles when injecting drugs. But heterosexuals generally? Only if they were incredibly unlucky, like that poor American girl who got deliberately infected by an evil gay dentist on a mission to make a political point.

Sure you can see why the gay community might have wanted to talk up the disease as a universal one. ("Everybody has AIDS" as the Broadway hit has it in *Team America*). Last thing they needed were finger-pointing straights ("Breeders") claiming it was God's judgment. Besides, if it were written off as a minority illness, how could it possibly compete for funding with cancer or heart disease?

You can see too why the media might have bought the "Everybody has AIDS" line. Nothing sells newspapers like a really juicy scare story, but to be scary, scare stories need to involve everyone, not just young men who do unsavory things to one another in bath houses.

What's less comprehensible—and certainly less excusable—is that our governments allowed this gay propaganda to affect their policy. They lied to us. They told us that AIDS was a disease for everyone, when it wasn't.

Why would they do that? Well maybe partly it was expediency: easier to prepare a "you are all at risk" blanket campaign than one that mentions unmentionable details like anal intercourse. Partly, they may not have yet been aware of the full picture: it was the early days, they needed to shoot first and ask questions later;

and governments do love hysteria, don't they, as it gives them lots of new programs to promote and money to spend, and a perfect excuse of "we told you so" if things go tragically wrong and people start falling in the streets. But mostly it was about government sucking up to (and caving into) minority interest groups, and in the process of trying to make things better actually make things a whole lot worse.

You might think I have an axe to grind against homosexuals. I don't. One of my best friends is gay and HIV positive, but being sensible and right-wing ("There just aren't enough bullets" is his favorite phrase) he'd never dream to suggest that his problem was one that should be shared by the broader society. He got the disease doing things (in a heavy-duty gay club) that heterosexuals tend not to do. Ergo, why, my friend would ask, should the state act as if they did?

The standard liberal defense of this kind of "well-meaning" state intervention goes something like this: sometimes, in order to protect the interests of vulnerable minorities, the state has to act against the interests of the majority. This, they believe, is what enlightened governments do.

I say no. I say that a government's duty—except under very special circumstances: vital military secrets, for example—is to tell the people who are funding it with their hard-earned tax dollars the truth. Even if that truth is an unpalatable one, it is far better that as free individuals the people are trusted to make up their own minds what to think than to have the government make up their minds for them.

Obviously I have an axe to grind here. You know I do. It is my contention that thanks to the lies told to my country by my government (a conservative government, too, which only confirms me in my view that all governments, not just left-wing ones, tend towards disaster) that I did not get to sleep with nearly as many nubile girls as I deserved to. In the Sixties they had free love; in the Seventies they had hippie, druggy love; in the Nineties they had Ecstasy love; in the Noughties you can find sex wherever you want on the Internet. Only the Eighties generation—my generation—missed out because of all that misinformation given by the state to credulous girls who otherwise, no doubt, would very happily have slept with me. Ignorance didn't kill me. Abstinence almost did.

To say that my life has been ruined thereby would be an exaggeration. But I still can't help feeling bitter that as I totter slowly towards old age, one of the great consolations of senescence will have been all but denied me. Elderly men and women from other, luckier, generations will be able to sit back contentedly in their armchairs and allow their thoughts to drift merrily through each and every one of the myriad sexual adventures they enjoyed in their misspent youth. It will keep them happy for hours, perhaps days on end. In my case it will last all of five minutes.

So I've given you the micro explanation for how Leftist ideology killed my sex life. Now I'll give you the macro one, which has been every bit as damaging as those misleading AIDS commercials and which will almost certainly have afflicted you as much as it has me. I refer to the insidious left-wing propaganda that has very successfully managed to persuade the world—especially the young, pretty, most sexually active part of the world—that all right-wing people are guilty of crimes including all or most of the following:

Crap taste in music; even worse taste in clothes; uselessness in bed; wanton sexism; casual racism; a taste for semi-auto-asphyxiation while masturbating with an orange stuck in your mouth (such as we had in the case of one young misguided Tory politician who accidentally killed himself doing this); insider dealing; extreme selfishness; environmental vandalism; philistinism; greed; stupidity; cruelty; mendacity; corruption; closed-mindedness; arms-dealing; extremism; bigotry; and pure, unvarnished evil.

Now apart maybe from the pure, unvarnished evil part—you girls do love a bastard, don't you?—are these really the kind of attributes likely to persuade a tender, sensitive young woman to share room-space with a man? I think not. Definitely not in my experience. What she'd much rather engage with—and who could blame her?—is the kind of guy who is: Devil-may-care; raffishly tousled; great in the sack; sexy; and cool.

The kind of guy who furthermore:

Sympathizes with the underdog; hates injustice; respects the ordinary working man (and woman); never discriminates against anyone regardless of their looks, race, sex (or "gender" as they're likely to call it), physical ability, or sexual preference; nurtures the environment; has great taste in music; opposes war and all forms of fascist aggression; is kind to children and small furry animals with lovely bright eyes and cute floppy ears, and expressions on their sweet pink little mouths you could damn near mistake for a human smile.

A left-wing person, in other words.

It's a no-brainer, isn't it? No wonder the voting habits of the younger generation tend so disproportionately towards the Left.

Not that I'm accusing young people of cynically adjusting their politics purely so they can get laid. Of course that's not the *only* reason. The herd mentality has a lot to do with it too. So does fashion and role-modelling.

Suppose you're young and impressionable and you're looking for an example of the kind of girl or guy who's going to help you make sense of this crazy political world, who you are going to choose?

George W. Bush, Dick Cheney, Chuck Norris, Ted Nugent, Newt Gingrich (the very name sounds like something that crawled out of a swamp), Tom DeLay, Dick Morris (a prostitute-frequenting political mercenary, for Heaven's sake!), and John McCain.

Or: Brad Pitt, Liv Tyler, Gwyneth Paltrow, Leonardo DiCaprio, George Clooney, Sheryl Crow, Jon Stewart, Barack Obama, and pretty much everyone else who's famous and desirable in the movies, on TV, in literature, in music, in political polemic, in every field in fact—save possibly sport—about which any young person is likely to give a damn.

But hey, look, I'm writing this book to console and reassure you not to make you feel worse. What you need to remind yourself is this: just because 99 percent of the world's most beautiful, glamorous people—and 99.99 percent of the ones featured on the cover of *Vanity Fair*—think the opposite to the way I do doesn't mean I'm an ugly person. Or an evil person. Or a wrong person.

It doesn't. Really it doesn't. The fact that we inhabit a world—it was bad enough even before Obama came to power, so imagine how much worse it's going to be now that the enemy has captured both houses of Congress—where most of our media, our seats of learning, our entertainers, our role models all seem to be singing from the same, drearily left-wing hymn sheet is not a reflection of justice or truth. It is merely a function of the Left's slippery cunning.

Blame, if you like, the influential Italian Marxist Antonio Gramsci, who in the early twentieth century formed the devious—and spot-on correct—theory that in order to win the political war, the Left would first have to win the cultural one. So it was that leftist firebrands who might once have gone into politics instead infiltrated the newspapers, the theatres, the seats of learning—anywhere where they could disseminate their ideology—and most successfully poisoned the minds of several generations.

Then again, you could as well argue that it was all going to happen anyway. There's a saying that if you're not a socialist when you're twenty you're heartless and if you're not a capitalist by the time you're forty you're brainless. I never went through the first stage myself, but I can see why a lot of young people do. It's because at that age, you've had next to no experience to form a judgement and because your drink-addled, drug-twisted, and hormonally-warped brain is especially prone to flights of crazed idealism.

Of course you're going to be drawn to a political philosophy which derives its primacy from feelings. Feelings at that tender age are the only thing you know. Why do so many models join PETA? Why did Jane Fonda go to Hanoi? Why does Leo DiCaprio lecture us about global warming?

Why do you think? Because it's just the sort of thing you do when you're led by the heart not the brain.

Some of us, most of us, grow out of this adolescent phase. Instead of formulating an idea of how the world ought to work and then trying to squeeze reality till it screams, we adopt a more mature, pragmatic approach. We look first at how the real world operates and base our schemes for improving it not on wishful thinking but on precedent and practicability.

It's never an easy thing, knowing you're right when so many other people out there are wrong. Especially when you know that cleaving to the truth may have cost you about 60 percent of the sexual partners you could have had. But in these dark and difficult times we're just going to have to learn to take our consolations where we can. The philosophy of the age may be one of arrested adolescence. But we're grown ups. We can take it. And youth doesn't last forever.

Chapter Three

THE ENVY OF THE WORLD

I **USED TO ENVY YOU AMERICANS** for your medical care. You have the best doctors, the best hospitals, the best medical research in the world. You're free, more or less, to choose what doctors you want; you have private, efficient "urgent care" doctors' offices dotted around your cities and towns; you don't have to wait five years to see a surgeon; and your dentists seem to be rather better than ours.

But all that's going to change.

Obama is going to bring you socialized medicine (though he'll call it something else)—and won't you be happy.

Of course I should never have been envious in the first place. "The Envy of the World." That's how people in Britain describe the NHS (National Health Service) our "free" universal healthcare system. And sometimes, even today, they manage to do it without a rueful shake of their head and a malevolent, ironic cackle.

Usually, it'll be in the letters columns of the newspaper, the day after the paper has run a story that goes something like this (stories you'll soon see in your own newspapers, if Obama and the Democrats have their way):

- Husband found by wife lying in same filthy sheets he vomited on when admitted to hospital two days before
- Hospital cleaners decide they find it more convenient to rinse infected drinking cups with cold water than to wash them with hot, soapy water
- Chief-Executive of hospital where 90 patients have died of infection due to dirty, blood-spattered wards gets $600,000 pay-off
- NHS $20 billion supercomputer breaks down 110 times in four months
- Government claims to have reduced waiting lists discovered to be result of fraudulent hospital figure-fiddling
- Patient complaints increase by 45 percent from 95,000 per year in 2004 to 138,000 in 2006
- Billions of pounds wasted on Private Finance Initiative hospital-building programs: businesses cream crazy profits by ripping off UK government; taxpayer in debt for next 125 years
- Redundant head of strategic health authority gets $1,450,000 pay off package described by one MP as "a lottery win rather than a pay out"
- Parents of 18-month child killed as a result of NHS negligence offered $20,000 in compensation
- 100,000 Alzheimer's suffers told NHS cannot afford $4 a day for drugs to alleviate their condition

- Study finds NHS managers waste up to $750 million paying far too much for drugs
- 50 Britons every day lose their sight to Age Related Macular Degeneration because local health authority refuses to treat them
- Nigerian visitor seeks heart transplant at British taxpayer's expense. Annual cost to NHS of "health tourism" estimated at between 50 million and 200 million pounds
- One in 300 of British hospital deaths is the result of a patient contracting an infection completely unrelated to the one for which they were admitted

I could go on but you get the idea. And you'll get an even better one when President Obama's lavish new universal healthcare program cranks into gear. He says it's going to cost you between $50 billion and $65 billion. If it costs you anything less than ten times that amount, then I'm Dr. Howard Dean's hairy right testicle. His left one too: I'm that confident.

Anyway, as I say, what invariably happens after one of these wearisomely familiar stories about NHS wastage, incompetence, malpractice, mismanagement, cover-ups, political-correctness, cheese-paring, criminal extravagance, or Augean disgustingness runs in the newspaper, is that there'll be some follow-up correspondence in the letters column. It'll say something like:

"Sir,

Your story yesterday about the ruptured waste pipe in Upton Snodsbury Hospital which sprayed patients in one ward for nearly two days before any of the hospital staff noticed gives a completely one sided picture of our wonderful NHS. Earlier this week my daughter gave birth in hospital, and I have nothing but the highest admiration for the professionalism and kindliness of the doctors and nurses, who made her stay a most pleasant one, and delivered her baby—my first grandson—with an efficiency and good humour which leaves me in no doubt that our NHS and its hardworking staff are still the Envy of the World."

All right, I exaggerate. Upton Snodsbury doesn't have a hospital and even if it did, I'm sure the cleaners would have spotted the ruptured sewage pipe within 36 hours, not 48. The general tone, though, is pretty much spot on. It's the authentically cowed, pathetically grateful voice of the client state, of a people who have lived so long under the "there's your gruel. Now be grateful for what you've got" spirit of socialism that they no longer fully understand what service and quality and value for money mean.

Before Margaret Thatcher came along and turned Britain from a second-rate Albania into something approaching a first world state, things were even worse. The whole of Britain's dying, mostly State-run industry, was in hock to the trade unions. If you bought a car, it rusted and fell to bits. If you wanted a telephone installed, you had to go on a three-month waiting list, then be ever-so, ever-so nice to the engineer who came to put it in, in case he didn't like you and changed his mind. These sound like tales from Ceaucescu's Romania, Honecker's East Germany, Kim Jong-il's North Korea but socialism is only Communism with slightly shorter queues.

"Whingeing Poms" the Australians call us, because we Brits are apparently always complaining so much. But if you ask me, we don't complain enough. I watched a TV documentary once about fruit. (Quiet evening, I suppose it must have been.) What I learned was that Europe's fruit wholesalers always send their crappiest peaches and nectarines and apricots to Britain because they know we'll take them, whereas any other country would send them back in disgust.

It's something to do with wartime rationing I guess, that whole "mustn't grumble" spirit of "make do and mend." When the national idea of a luxury dinner becomes something called Woolton Pie—that's potatoes, cauliflower, rutabaga, carrots, turnips, and rolled oats cooked with thickened vegetable water and coated with potato pastry, as recommended by the wartime Minister of Food—I suppose you do get out of the habit of demanding your steak well-hung, medium-rare, with a side-order of *foie gras* and grated truffle.

You see what I mean, though, about that typical kindly Englishman who has written his letter to the newspaper about how great the NHS is? His appreciation comes from such a low critical base as to be absolutely meaningless.

"But what did you expect?" you want to ask the guy. "Nurses screaming in patients' ears and trying to claw out their eyes? Doctors with massive rubber truncheons battering the soles of patients' feet so the bruises don't show? Piles of rotting corpses in the corridors? Cockroaches in the porridge? This is supposed to be a hospital, for God's sake, not the torture complex of a prison in Equatorial Guinea. These doctors and nurses you're so impressed with. You do realize they're paid for this be-nice-to-patients, make-them-feel-better and not-kill-their-babies schtick? You realize they probably entered the profession in the first place because they were already of a healing, caring, disposition? Otherwise, they'd have chosen a different career path. Serial killing maybe."

(This is not to say that serial killing and British medical care are wholly incompatible. Witness the spectacular success of our Dr. Harold Shipman, the respected family doctor from Yorkshire, jailed for life in 2000 for having killed at least 215 of his patients by lethal injection. It was, of course, wholly characteristic of NHS effiency that he was able to manage this murder spree, completely undetected, over a period of three years.)

Kindly he may be, this imaginary Englishman who wrote that stupid letter. But it's him—or real people like him—who must bear a chunk of the blame for the grudging, half-cocked treatment we get in our hospitals.

Take the time, a few years ago, I was at a wedding in Wales and I fell into a ha-ha. Falling into a ha-ha isn't funny. A "ha-ha" is a deep ditch that British grandees used to dig in their gardens, at the point where the manicured lawn of their vast country pile meets the grazing land beyond. The idea of the ditch is to keep the animals from the estate encroaching on the garden, while at the same time tricking the eye, when looking outwards from house, into thinking that the lawn merges seamlessly with the oak-studded parkland beyond. That's why it's called a "ha-ha": because you don't notice it, till you've fallen into it.

So there I am, walking with my wife across the lawn towards the marquee we can see in the parkland beyond, when suddenly the ground disappears from beneath our feet. It's like something from a nightmare. Utter disorientation. The plunge through space that seems to last a lifetime. Then the realization that things aren't at all right. You're shaking. You're distressed. You can't move.

"Come on!" says my wife, whose inner feline has enabled her to survive the twelve foot drop into a narrow, wet ditch completely unscathed.

"I can't," I say.

"Don't be silly!" she snaps, sympathetic as she always is whenever I'm ill.

"I can't."

"What's the matter? Come on! We need to get back to the party. It's not broken, is it?"

"I don't know," I say, shaking.

My ankle is in fact broken. But we don't discover this till at least three hours later. It's not the drive from deepest rural Wales to a hospital that takes the time. It's the NHS system. First you must be processed by a miserable, pasty-faced receptionist—not immediately, of course: she has important business to complete, filing her nails, finishing off her Sudoku puzzle, putting in a quick call to her friend about their clubbing arrangements after work—who treats you with a practiced contempt she makes no attempt to hide.

"How dare you waste my time, like this? Who do you think you are? Don't you realize I have a job to do?" her body language shrieks as she tuttingly hands you the forms to fill in. Death, they say, is the great social leveller. And for the living, there's the British hospital: probably the one chance a tax-paying, law-abiding citizen gets to appreciate how it feels being admitted to prison or going to claim welfare. "And I'm PAYING for this treatment?" you wonder disbelievingly.

But worse is to come. Now you must wait a minimum of an hour, on bad nights three or four, before you get any treatment for your misery and pain. You sit in a crowded waiting area, beneath flickering yellow strip lighting, with nothing to do save gaze agog (while pretending not to, of course, for personal safety reasons) at the specimens of humanity who'll be joining you on your slow passage towards the gates of hell. It makes the cantina scene from *Star Wars* look like *High School Musical III*.

And this isn't just a snob thing going on here. No, that's a lie. Of course it's a snob thing. These are mostly the kind of people you'd run a mile to avoid in the course of your normal daily life. Drunks reeking of alcohol and stale ordure; young thugs who've been stabbed in knife fights; palpitating, wild-eyed, sweating immigrants who look like they might be carrying something tropical, deadly, and highly contagious.

What's interesting, though, is how quickly this snob thing gives way to group solidarity. United through boredom, suffering, and frustration at the grinding slowness of the system, these strangers become for those next few hours almost like friends. Comrades in arms, at any rate. You swap stories about how you came to be here. You become especially concerned for those patients—that probable Ebola case for example—who haven't yet been seen, but damned well ought to be, and fast. A socialist would argue that this budding, classless camaraderie, almost in itself, is justification enough for the NHS. I wouldn't. If I have to go to hospital I want to get medical treatment, not have my consciousness raised. But hey, I'm a conservative. That's just the kind of selfish bastard I am.

Sure it's good for the soul, this brothers-and-sisters-under-the-skin, enforced love-in that takes place in an NHS waiting room. But it doesn't half grate on the intelligence. You sit there amid all this misery and squalor and you think to yourself: "I am not an unreasonable, particularly uncaring person. I've never used the phrase 'Don't you know who I am?' And I've always believed in basic, safety-net healthcare provision for the poor, both for reasons of Christian charity and for social harmony. Yes, I'm really glad to live in a world where the indigent no longer die on the doorsteps of the callous rich, where working class mothers no longer waddle the cobbled Northern streets with prolapsed uteruses dangling between their legs because there's no money spare for doctors when you've seven children to feed. . . . "

"But," you go on—and it really is a big important but, so perhaps it should be in capital letters—"BUT what kind of justice is it where, despite having paid for far more than my share of this system through my taxes, I STILL get treated like I'm some scrounging, unworthy supplicant?"

This is something you'll hear very few British people ever admit. They've been too thoroughly brainwashed by all those years of "envy of the world" propaganda. They're too sentimentally smitten by this wonderful notion that the NHS is and always will be "free healthcare provided at the point of need." It's why not even the Tories will dare campaign any more on a ticket which in any way seems to threaten this sclerotic, grotesquely inefficient, mind-bogglingly expensive healthcare system devised by a socialist in the 1940s for a world that has changed immeasurably since.

Any incoming Republican administration is going to have similar difficulties unravelling President Obama's version thereof. Once these tax-leeching Behemoths are in place, you're stuck with the ravening beast for good.

And boy do these monsters eat up money. In 2007–2008 the British National Health Service swallowed up 95 billion pounds—more than any other government department. (Education got 73 billion pounds; 34 billion pounds was spent on Defense.) For this, the taxpayer gets a "service" so lamentably poor that 55 percent of senior doctors pay for private medical insurance rather than run the risk of having to expose themselves to the NHS's tender cares.

Who would blame them, either, when NHS hospitals are now estimated to be responsible for around 40,000 patient deaths a year? That's 5,000 more deaths than resulted from civil war violence in Iraq in 2006. In an international study of "mortality amenable to healthcare," Britain came last out of 19 countries surveyed. It is estimated that at least 30,000 of the 200,000 people who die from cancer or strokes each year in Britain would survive if treated in any other European country. (For further shocking examples I highly recommend *Squandered* by David Craig, which analyzes in terrifying detail the 1,299,100,000,000 pounds wasted over a period of 11 years by the British Labour government.)

You'll say, the more optimistic among you, that America's version will be different. Obama will get it right. Well he couldn't get it any more wrong than we Brits have done, that's for certain. But the moment you set up a state healthcare system you run into at least one intractable problem. The big clue is in that word "state."

Quite simply, government can never run any service as efficiently as private enterprise can. For one thing, it operates on a scale which is too unwieldy. The British National Health Service is the world's largest employer after the Chinese army and the Indian State Railway: any CEO would tell you, this takes you way beyond economies of scale into the wilder purlieus of Cloudcuck-ooland.

More dangerously for the taxpayer who must fund it, it is not subject to market discipline. However harsh the capitalist system may be, at least you know where you stand. The bottom line is money which is the root, not only of all evil, but also—suck on this, socialist scum!—the root of all rational business decisions, efficiency, and consumer benefit.

So, for example, it is in the interests of a privately run hospital to: keep its costs down (if not it will lose business to cheaper rivals); be nice to its patients and try to kill as few of them as possible (prospective customers can be very fussy that way); feed them food that isn't pigswill (see above); treat patients quickly, change their dirty sheets, scrub blood off the walls, wipe out the roaches (see also above). And, of course, to refuse to treat patients who aren't going to pay.

To the socialist mindset, that last detail constitutes a crime almost against humanity. Health, he would argue, is not a luxury but a fundamental Human Right, enshrined—see Article 25, Universal Declaration of Human Rights—by UN Charter. Where, though, the rest of us might reasonably wonder, does one person's inalienable right to medical treatment on all occasions and at whatever cost begin, and another person's right to choose exactly how he spends his hard-earned bucks end?

And if the Human Right to health really is that fundamental where does this leave us on "health tourism"? Presumably, as a citizen of the world, I am supposed to welcome with open arms all those ailing Nigerian women who might wish to fly over for $100,000 heart transplant surgery courtesy of my national health service. Is their right to life any less great than yours or mine?

This is exactly the sort of question we should NOT be asking where something as expensive as healthcare is concerned. Not, indeed, the sort of question we should be asking where pretty much *anything* is concerned, because it muddies the issue, takes everything down to the level of cheap (or rather very costly) emotionalism at which socialist ideologues so excel.

Yeah, yeah, of course, if any of us were to get to know one of these Nigerian women, of course we'd want to her to get "free" heart treatment at our country's expense. We'd find out how much her kids loved and needed her; how she was the apple of her parents' eye; how pitiful it was that a woman so young should yet find herself so enfeebled by this awful heart complaint. We'd care, we'd want to help because that's just the kind of people most of us are. We want good stuff to happen to people we know. Not bad stuff. (Well, providing they're not our enemies, that is...)

One of the things, I've noticed, that we Europeans are always trying to make you Americans feel guilty about is the alleged harshness built into your medical system. We say how disgraceful it is that if you get knocked over by a car in the Land of the Free the emergency services *won't even touch you* till they've seen your medical insurance details. And some of you, the self-hating liberal ones which for some reason are the type you mostly get to meet in London, go: "Gee you're so right. What a heartless, fascist nation that makes us."

No it doesn't. What it makes you is a grown-up nation: one that has wrestled with a morally contentious problem and come up with the only fair and just answer. You offer minimum, safety-net healthcare to those who have no other option, (and I gather you treat more than your fair share of illegal immigrants who can't afford to pay either). And for every one else, you remove the distorting effects of sentiment from the equation, by letting money decide. The more money you pay, the better quality of service you get—just as you do with restaurants, or automobiles, or vacations, or any of the other goods and services available in our intrinsi-cally-unfair-but-nonetheless-fairer-than-any-other-system-man-has-yet-devised capitalist society.

This is one of the bitter thoughts that strikes me as I sit in the waiting area of that Welsh hospital, my broken ankle really starting to hurt me now, and still with no immediate prospect of treatment. I think: "I have a job I don't always enjoy. I work hard for my money. Damned hard. I don't earn as much as I'd like. And much of what I do earn gets taken me from the government. There's not a single person waiting in this room who contributes as much to the economy as I do. Sure they're human beings, as I am, with thoughts and feelings and loved ones, and so on, but still let's cut to the chase here. Some of them pay only a tiny bit of tax. Most I'm guessing don't pay any tax at all. A percentage of them, aren't even European citizens eligible for treatment. So how come, as far as this crappy hospital is concerned, I'm no better than they are?"

And it's not that I'm being tight-fisted, by the way. I do have medical insurance. (Limited, admittedly: here, as it is in the United States, it doesn't come cheap.) But in this cottage hospital in the middle of Wales—with no other one anywhere nearby offering emergency treatment facilities—my medical insurance makes no difference. Nor does money. At one point, when the pain gets almost too much to bear, and all they've given me is a couple of low-dose painkillers (such as you might use to treat a slight headache, not a fractured ankle for Heaven's sake), I hobble over to the receptionist and say: "Look. I need proper pain relief. I'm happy to pay for it." The receptionist says (with evident inner joy at my discomfort): "No. The NHS makes no provision for that kind of additional service."

The wait goes on. My bitter thoughts continue: "So in almost every other area of my life, I'm considered mature and responsible enough to allocate my budget. If I'm feeling flush I can go to the Ivy; if poor, I can stay at home; I can decide whether to spend every last available penny sending my kids to private school, or enjoy a lot more comfortable life by sending them to a state one.

Yet when it comes to maybe the most important area of all—my physical well-being—I am no longer a free agent. It is for the State to decide, how much pain I suffer, how long I must wait before I am treated, whether or not the wards in which I'm treated are infested with antibiotic-resistant viruses (MRSAs) which could ruin my life forever."

You still wonder what my beef is with socialism?

Here's another story, one concerning my dear mother-in-law, Rose, who died a few years ago in her Eighties. In England we're all supposed to hate our mothers-in-law (hence jokes like: Wife: There's a burglar downstairs eating that cake my mother made. Husband: Who shall I call? The police or an ambulance?) but I always adored mine.

It helped, of course, that she was always laughing at my jokes and saying how clever my articles were. But mainly it was because she was gentle and warm, stoical and civilized and harked back to another, better age. As a child, she rode to hounds (the last thing she did before she died was present me with her father's silver edged hunting crop) and lived in a big house with servants. Like many upper class English girls of her generation, she never did a day's work in her life, apart from during the war where she worked at Bletchley Park, the famous code-breaking centre with the Enigma machine. In her youth she was a tremendous beauty, and retained her vitality and looks right to the end, swimming every day.

Then quite suddenly, she began to fall apart. It was awful to watch. You expect people so hale and fit to go on forever. One day this splendidly stoical woman was in such pain she did something she'd never normally do and screamed in agony. My father-in-law called the ambulance. The crew tried to help her downstairs but she was in too much pain to move. Until recently, they would have been able to carry her down. But this, they explained, would now put them in breach of European Health and Safety regulations.

They would have to call for special equipment. It was another hour before this special equipment arrived—an hour in which my mother-in-law's "health and safety" might better have been served in hospital, rather than doubled-up on the floor of her sitting room, screaming.

Some weeks later she died. It cannot have been an edifying experience for a woman of her background and generation being stuck in a mixed sex hospital ward where the only privacy was the curtain round your bed, where the nurses insisted on addressing you in the modern way by your first name, and where the food was disgusting to the point of inedibility. Still she bore it with the stoicism you'd expect of the wartime generation.

After Christmas, she took a turn for the worse, and with hindsight it seems obvious she was never going to recover. A cancer had been found in her bladder; she'd been infected by necrotising fasciitis (caught in the hospital presumably); whatever the outcome, she was doomed never again to enjoy the active life she had before. Her last days were spent on a life support machine in intensive care, battling the inevitable. The consultant told us that there was one last trick he was going to try. An injection, each shot of which cost 2,000 pounds. I think he gave her two of these. They bought my mother-in-law—what?—six to eight hours more of squalid, wheezing, oxygen-pumped, saline-dripped non-existence before she was permitted the succour of death.

At the time there were lots of stories in the papers about how high the NHS's deficit was. 200 million pounds? 200 *billion* pounds? Silly money, at any rate. Debts of such astronomical vastness you couldn't even begin to guess where the Government might find the extra money.

And as the young consultant was telling us about these shots he was going to give her, exulting in how expensive they were, I joked something like: "Gosh. That's not going to do much for your department's book-balancing this week."

To which the consultant replied something like: "What do I care? We're a hospital, not a supermarket."

Which is yet another reason why any state healthcare system is a disaster waiting to happen. This consultant, he's a caring guy, and he's taken the Hippocratic Oath. His primary duty as he sees it is to keep his patients alive at almost any cost. If he was interested in figures he would have become an accountant, not a doctor. In his heart, he knows it's an abomination that anything so vulgar as money should creep into the equation when something as valuable as a human life is at stake.

That's why he chose to work in the state sector, not the private one. He may get paid less money but, like a lawyer working pro bono, this puts him on the side of the angels. It lends weight to his moral certitude that no money is too much money to spend on a dying old woman. It also means that the size of his salary (fixed according to a sliding government pay scale) is completely disconnected from concerns that might affect someone subject to the market disciplines of the private sector. Concerns like patient satisfaction, productivity, or efficiency.

But hey, is that not as it should be? The sanctity of human life, and all that? Well no—in my evil conservative way, I fear I must beg to differ. Look, I've told you how very much I loved my mother-in-law. I did, I really did. And I wish she was still here, being a mother to my wife, a wife to her husband, a grandmother to my children—but only on the terms she would have wanted which is fit and healthy and mobile, not attached to a bag or stuck in a wheelchair. The question in this case was not doctor-assisted suicide, which is another issue altogether, but recognizing when it is in no one's best interest to pursue extraordinary, and likely futile, means to keep someone alive. That's why when all's said and done I think that consultant made the wrong call. It was probably wrong in absolute terms—because I suspect by that stage poor Rose was a lost cause. It was definitely wrong in relative terms, because in a cash-starved system of finite resources, the 4,000 pounds wasted on those injections could certainly have been better spent elsewhere. On kids with their whole life ahead of them maybe. Or a year's drugs relief for two Alzheimer's sufferers.

This "finite resources" concept is something I don't think the Left has ever grasped. Not about health care. Not about anything where its demands for state spending is concerned. (Except defense of course. The Left has always displayed a huge sense of unwonted fiscal responsibility in the matter of defense). The State, being richer than any other entity in the land, is considered fair game for anything. It's like your favorite rich uncle—the guy with the bottomless pockets.

His pockets aren't really bottomless, of course. It's just a question of perspective. Because he lives in a bigger house in a ritzier neighbourhood than you and drives a smarter car than you, you assume he's got money to burn. You imagine he's so rich, in fact, that he's not even subject to the budgetary considerations ordinary folk like you are. Once, when you were fetching something from his study, you caught sight of his monthly pay-slip, or one of his dividend payments, and you thought: "Wow! My uncle is rich like I would never have believed. When I touched him for 500 bucks the other day, I felt kind of guilty about it. But now I wish I had touched him for a thousand—and next time I will!"

If ever you had the guts to raise this with your uncle, he'd probably sit you down and take you through his accounts. He'd show you his tax bill, and the bills for heating and cleaning the pool, and the cost of the gardener, and the service bills for the staff, and the golf club fee, and all the other rich-person's-lifestyle bills which, while not exactly making you feel sorry for him, would at least teach you an important lesson. No one—well, almost no one—is ever so rich that they don't have to spend time worrying about how best to allocate their resources. And actually, you didn't need your rich uncle to tell you this. If you'd thought a bit harder, you could have put yourself in the position of all the people below you in the socio-economic scale and tried to imagine how they think about you.

Yes, exactly. They regard you with just the same mix of avarice and jealousy with which you regard your favorite rich uncle. They go: "Well it's all right for him. He doesn't ever have to worry where the next cent is coming from. He never has to budget...." And if ever you overheard them saying this, you'd go: "Whaaat? They can't mean me? Surely they can't mean me. Don't they have ANY IDEA what a struggle it is to pay the school fees/heating bills/car insurance...?"

On and on this pettifogging bitterness and misunderstanding goes, down the socio-economic scale, almost ad infinitum. And if some of us didn't know better it would make class warriors of us all and keep the Democrats in power till the end of time. A lot of us, of course, don't know better, which is why a socialist huckster like Obama can make such mighty political capital out of statements like "It is time for folks like me who make more than $250,000 to pay our fair share."

Fair? Sweet Heaven there we go again. "Fair" used in its exquisitely nuanced socialist context of "Not fair at all." According to the latest Internal Revenue Service figures, the top one percent of U.S. taxpayers already pay 40 percent of all income taxes. And the top 10 percent of income earners pay 71 percent of taxes. In my book that's not just unfair. That's cruel and unusual punishment.

The reason Obama can get away with this, of course, is that there are rather more U.S. citizens who think a $250,000 plus salary qualifies you for rich uncle status than there are U.S. citizens who think of it as a bare, living wage. But this is not about equity. And it's certainly not about economic sense: not when every study there has ever been shows that when you reduce taxes for high-earners the economy grows and everyone, not just the rich, benefits. Rather it's about exploiting some of the lumpen majority's most ignoble impulses—jealousy, resentment, a sense of entitlement—and repackaging them under the more flattering title "Equity" or "Social Justice."

But I digress. No, actually I don't digress at all, because this issue of taxation cuts to the heart of the state healthcare issue. I said before—and it's so shocking it can't be stated often enough—that of all the areas to which the British taxpayer's money is diverted, our National Health Service is by some way the largest. It eats up more than Defense, more than Education, more than any other single British government department. Is it not right, then, that the taxpayer should benefit from this arrangement? I think so. Wouldn't you?

Instead, we have a system so bad—well let me tell you one more story to show just how bad it is. It's late last autumn, the temperatures have started to drop to the point where my desire to save money on heating bills is finally trumped by my desire not to die of hypothermia, and I am crouched on the floor of our kitchen trying to relight the gas oven we turned off for the duration of the summer.

The oven is called a Rayburn and it's one of our proudest possessions. It's an old-fashioned range cooker and every civilized British family aspires to owning one—or its better-known sister, the Aga—because it's redolent of so many of things the British adore: wet Labradors, bubbling pots of home made soup, tea made from big kettle warmed on the hob, by-gone ages generally. But they are, as we say in England, a bugger to light.

No, that's not fair. They're not a bugger to light so long as you read the instructions. But on this occasion I am in no mood to read the instructions, for I am a man, and having done it successfully before this time last year I refuse to waste valuable time re-reading instructions when instead I can simply hurl myself into the breach and just get on with it.

"Are you sure the gas is meant to be hissing like that?" says my wife anxiously, watching from a considerable distance. She knows that do-it-yourself handyman work has never been my forte. I can't even change a plug, but if I don't do this, we'll only have to call in our Polish plumber to do it. And that will cost money whereas if I do it, it's free. "Yeah yeah. It's fine," I say, reaching for another match. The first one got blown out by the force of the gas. Not sure I remember it being quite like this last year. Ah well, so long as I can get the thing lit before TOO much leaking gas accumulates in the atmosphere, I'm sure it'll all be okay.

I light another match and stick my hand deeper inside the oven.

"I think you should stop. This doesn't sound right," says my wife.

"Oh stop worrying. I know what I'm—"

WHUMPPP!

It's so horrible, so unreal it's like one of those things that happens to other people but never you.

I've been physically thrown backwards by the explosion. There's a strong smell of singed hair. I can feel the crispy, burnt stubble where my eyelashes used to be. And when I look down at my hand, it doesn't look at all right. In fact it looks so ghastly that I have to look away. Then I look back again because I can't resist checking to see whether it really does look as bad as I thought it did. And it does.

Instead of being nice and pink, all the skin on my right hand has turned a shrivelled silvery-white color. It feels all tight, like I'm wearing an undersized rubber glove. Underneath that tightness, I can also feel the first inkling of very great pain.

Oh my God. What do I do? This can't be happening! What do I do?

I rush over to the kitchen sink, turn on the faucet, and leave my hand under the cold running water. The pain is really starting to kick in now. The water isn't nearly cold enough to stop the agony. But when I try pulling my hand away, to see if I can cope with it outside the flow of cold water, I realize that it's quite impossible. Never have I experienced such intense, burning agony in all my life.

Okay. Enough horror detail, already. I'm telling you this story for a particular reason. And the reason is, because I want you to know what I do next.

What would you do next? You'd check yourself into your nearest hospital, soon as you could, right? You'd get a trained doctor to look at it, get yourself some pain relief, right?

Yes. That would indeed be the logical course of action in any half-way civilized country.

Not, however, in socialist Britain.

There's a massive hospital just ten minutes walk away from where I live. But I don't want to go there. I'll do almost anything to avoid going there.

My hand is on fire. I'm holding it under the tap, dancing a frenzied jig of pain and despair, while my wife hovers concernedly nearby.

But I still don't consider going to hospital. For the next half hour I do everything I can to try to avoid going to hospital. Holding the phone with my left hand, I call up friends who I think might know a doctor, friends who've done a bit of nursing, people who actually are doctors and they all say the same thing: "Check yourself into the nearest A & E" (Accident and Emergency).

It's sound advice. It's the only possible advice. But still I persist, and ring up more people in the hope that one of them's going to tell me what I really want to hear which is: "Naah. Just take a few painkillers and sleep it off. You'll be okay."

Eventually I surrender. I go to the hospital and everything pans out just as I feared it would: the long wait; the squalor; the *Star Wars* cantina scene; the surliness; the tedium; the despair.

The treatment I get at the end of it, three hours later, is pleasant and professional. I even get liquid morphine, which dulls most of the pain.

But that's not my point. My point is the Third Circle of Hell through which I had to pass in order to get this treatment.

Was there ever a more damning indictment of a socialist health-care system? The service so costly it eats up the biggest part of your tax dollar, but so terrible that even in your hour of greatest need, you'd rather walk barefoot across hot coals then ever have to use it.

That, my friends, is the health care of your Obamaland future.

Chapter Four

WHY SOCIALISTS HAVE NO CLASS

AMERICANS HAVE A HEALTHY AVERSION to the idea of government-enforced equality. When Joe the Plumber caught Obama out on his plans to "spread the wealth around" it was one of the few bright spots of the McCain campaign. Socialists are all for equality, of course, and so is Obama. They like to pose as class warriors, raiding the wealthy for the benefit of the poor. They want a "classless" society—getting rid of landed aristocrats like, say, George Washington and Thomas Jefferson—for the benefit of people who are content to be the government-succoured masses. And leading the charge will be those paragons of self-denial—folks like Al Gore, Michael Moore, and the Clintons.

Their bludgeon to ensure equality will be higher taxes. Obama will play the class card and target "the wealthy"—an elastic category of anyone who makes more money than he decides makes political sense. Higher taxes will fund all the big, new government programs Obama will assure us are necessary to ensure fairness and economic justice. To a socialist like Obama that means raiding the earnings of the most productive—you know, the people who actually produce wealth and would normally invest in new businesses and create new jobs—and giving it to dependents of the state.

Socialists can talk all they want about equality, but we've all read *Animal Farm* and we know it's not really equality they're after; the socialist masters themselves will always be more equal than others: Al Gore will always burn his way through more carbon credits and Michael Moore will always eat more hotdogs than the rest of us are allowed. No, what they hate, as our former Prime Minister Blair put it in one of his more unguarded speeches, are "the forces of conservatism." And they think the chief reactionary redoubt is among the wealthy, the Wall Street bankers, the successful entrepreneurs, the WASPy upper classes.

It's to that end that Obama thinks America needs more equality—and he's flat out wrong. To show you why—while simultaneously allowing me to drop the names of the Royal Family and to show off what ritzy friends I've got—let me invite you on a day's grouse-shooting in Scotland. (Don't worry, Obama's not coming with us. He's scared of guns.)

Have you ever been to the Scottish highlands in August? Awesome place, so long as you can cope with the midges. "No see-ums" they're sometimes called because they're virtually invisible. Soon as the wind drops, they're on to you, sucking like miniature vampires at every inch of exposed flesh, making your scalp itchy and bumpy, leaving little red blotches all over your face. And so evil too. They have a kind of collective intelligence—not unlike those huge black mosquitoes that lurk in packs in the parking lots in the Everglades, waiting for tourists to open their car doors—so that when one goes for you, her thousand and one sisters go for you too. In tourist surveys, 60 percent of first-time summer visitors to Scotland vow that they'll never return because of the midges.

Apart from the midges, though, the Scottish highlands in August are just great. Craggy peaks, gurgling streams ("burns"), rushing salmon rivers, vast herds of shaggy red deer scurrying along the sides of majestic valleys ("glens" as in the famous picture Queen Victoria's favorite animal painter Edwin Landseer did of a stag: "The Monarch of the Glen") variegated in such a gorgeous array of almost unreal colors it's like staring at a patchwork quilt on some kind of psychedelic trip.

The purple heather especially. It seems to glow at you, almost like neon, from the sides of the mountains. The greens too—they're so deep and fresh and vibrant it's like seeing green for the first time. Setting all this off is the grey of the rocks and any number of shades of brown from dun to russet to chocolate. And to complete the aura of unreality, the colors don't merge softly into one another as they do in your regular wild landscapes. Rather, they're divided into distinct blocks with defined edges—just like on that quilt I mentioned. There'll be an area of brown. Then an area of green. Then an area of darker green. Then an area of black. It looks as if each year the hillside has been ravaged by a series of mini fires, which have been put out just in time before they've had a chance to spread.

This indeed is exactly what has happened. Each year, the owners of this land will torch a different part of the heather moorland, as they have done for generations. And the reason for this is that they want to encourage the grouse, whose young like to feed on the tips of the young heather which pokes up in those areas which were burnt the previous year. The grouse (and the wild salmon, and the deer) are the landowners' livelihood. Without them—something the vindictive socialists in the Scottish parliament of course refuse to understand—they could never afford to maintain their vast, but agriculturally valueless estates, some of them like my friend Hamish's, extending thirty square miles.

Just a few valleys away from the one I'm looking down on now—shotgun in the crook of my elbow, midge repellant all over my skin—lies Balmoral Castle, summer resort of our royal family. They've been coming here since the nineteenth century when Queen Victoria and her consort Prince Albert developed their mad passion for the area. (Later, when Albert died, the Queen sought solace in the gruff, manly companionship of her stern ghillie—outdoor manservant—John Brown. Before her death she ordered a lock of his hair to be put in her coffin. There are rumors that they secretly married.)

You'd naturally assume that the royal family represented the very peak of the British class system, but this is not so. Members of the grander ducal families or the older English earldoms, still think of the royals as vulgar, mittel European arrivistes who only rolled up from the Continent just over three centuries ago, and who only changed their name from worryingly foreign-sounding Battenburg to the more English Windsor during the period of Germanophobia in the First World War.

The British class system has these super-subtle distinctions all the way through. Take my friend Hamish who is next in line to become the local laird, and chief of a Scottish clan. In the rest of Britain, a Scottish laird counts for squat against a Duke, a Marquess, an Earl, or even a relatively humble Lord. But back on his home turf—even in the grim socialist Misery State that Scotland has largely become these days now it has its own ultra-left parliament—he still has tremendous cachet. True, he no longer has the *droit de seigneurial* right at Highland festivals to pick the choicest young maids and have them brought to his draughty castle bedchamber, there to satisfy his every desire. But he does still get to wear an unusually spiffy sporran (that's the large ornamental

purse with the furry dangly bits which a Scotsman hangs sugges-
tively over his kilt directly in front of his crotch); he gets to wear
real eagle feathers in his Highland hat; he gets to sit right next to
the Queen at Highland games (caber tossing; hammer throwing;
etc); and, as clan chief, he is the titular head of all the families in
the world with his particular Scottish surname. McLaren, say. Or
Fergusson. Or Farquharson.

See what fun you're missing in your (supposedly) classless society?

Then there's me. You might think from the fact that I'm on a
Scottish moor doing something as spiffy as grouse-shooting—it's
probably the grandest, most expensive, and socially rarefied sport
in Britain, only available to the very few and costing upwards of
$10,000 per gun per day—that I'm a member of the upper classes.
But I'm not. I'm what in Britain would be termed middle class.
Upper middle class at a push. Definitely not a toff.

When I was at university at Oxford, surrounded by titled Old
Etonians, this used to bother me somewhat. Every day, I'd visit my
pigeon hole in the porter's lodge of my sumptuously grand college
Christ Church (alma mater of the poet W. H. Auden, the children's
author Lewis Carroll; not to mention thirteen British Prime Ministers and eleven Viceroys of India) in the hope that I'd find a letter saying something like this:

> Dear Mr. Delingpole, as Garter King of Arms, Lyon Rouge
> Pursuivant it is my honour to inform you that owing to the
> untimely death of your thirteenth-cousin-once-removed the 15th
> Duke of Wessex, you are now heir to the Dukedom, its five
> acres of prime residential and commercial property in London,
> its 5,000 acre estate in Wiltshire, its 300,000 acre grouse moor
> in Scotland, its pack of foxhounds, its buxom serving wenches,
> its yearly prerogative to consume ten of the Royal swans, and

all other money, land, property and appertenances applying thereto. As the Duke's—your father's—son-and-heir you are henceforward entitled to style yourself the Marquess of Tisbury.

"Ha! That'll show those snooty Old Etonians!" I used to mutter to myself. "Think I'm common do they? Think I don't count because I only went to a MINOR public school and my father makes nuts and bolts and talks with a faint Birmingham accent? Well how stupid are they all going to look now, eh? Now that they'll have to bow and scrape to me and BEG me for invitations to my palace, which of course I'm never going to give them unless they lick my boots and beg 'Oh please, please, please mighty and reverend Lord Tisbury. We were such fools to have ever doubted your greatness!'"

Unfortunately the letter never arrived and throughout my three years at Oxford—and right up to this day—I remained stubbornly James Delingpole, Esq., scion of a deeply unimportant Midlands industrial family whose only real distinction is to have a slightly unusual surname.

The difference between then and now is that it doesn't bother me any more. Not one bit. And the reason it doesn't bother me is because I've learned to appreciate that far from being restrictive, oppressive, and unjust, a strong class system—the very inequality that socialists hate—can be a wonderfully lithe, elastic, mobile thing which actually serves to make the world a better, happier and—yes—fairer place for everyone.

Consider this grouse shoot that I'm on now—eyes darting, trigger finger itching, midges biting, striding through the heather in some of the most beautiful scenery in all the world, counting my blessings that my smart friend Hamish has seen fit to invite a humble fellow like me on an actual Scottish pheasant shoot.

Ahead of me a sudden startled clucking. Five dark shapes burst upwards from the heather and accelerate rapidly into the distance.

Heart pounding, I raise my gun, trying to remember too many things at once—safety catch off; butt tight into the shoulder so the recoil doesn't bruise me; aim ahead of the birds not behind; make sure there are no people or dogs ahead of you—and squeeze the trigger, once then again. Blam! Blam! Amazing. Beginner's luck it, must be, for one of those dark shapes has dropped from the sky. "Well done, old boy. Bagged your first grouse!" says Hamish. His Ghillie sends his dog forward to fetch the still-flapping bird. Having broken its neck, he reaches into the gory cavity and ceremonially smears my face with blood. I am complete. I have joined the upper class.

Not really. It takes more than killing a grouse to do that. But why would you want to become a toff anyway? With title and land come tedium, duty, and responsibility. Far better, surely, to be able to just enjoy all the trappings of the toff lifestyle, without having to talk like you've got a plum in your mouth, manage truculent staff, behave at formal dinner like you've got a broom handle stuck up your you-know-where, and descend from a long line of inbreeds rife with madness, recklessness, infidelity, and suicidal depression?

Now I haven't yet explained to you the mystery of what it is that I—a mere middle-class scribbler with no money—am doing on this shoot. Am I having an affair with my host's wife? Am I a powerful person whose influence is worth courting? Am I an especially fine shot whose marksmanship is such a joy to watch that I'm deluged by invitations to shooting estates the length and breadth of the land? Am I an endless fund of hilarious anecdotes? Am I Hamish's secret catamite?

None of the above actually, though they would all be perfectly valid justifications. The reason I think I'm here—apart from the obvious one, that my host is a lovely chap who likes me—is that I'm a writer. Not a particularly famous one. But sufficiently well known in certain circles to be considered in some poor deluded fools' eyes a mildly interesting social catch. "You must come and meet our new friend James Delingpole," they can say to their friends. "You know, the one who does the TV column in the *Spectator*. Terribly right-wing, but quite funny with it sometimes."

Things have always been this way for writers. It's about the only thing the job has going for it. The money's crap. The hours are long. You spend far, far too much time on tortured self-examination. No one gives a damn. But occasionally, just occasionally, you'll hear from some sucker out there who holds you at your own estimation and thinks you're worth cultivating. In the old days, this was about the only way a starving artist could survive. Think Shakespeare and the Earl of Rochester; think the Medicis and most of the Renaissance. And in some ways it still is. "So what if no one reads my books. So what if I can't afford to educate my children. So what if my wife's perpetually on the verge of leaving me for someone with career prospects and a pension plan," you can say to yourself. "What matters is that right here, right now, I'm standing with a gun on a Scottish grouse moor, with one of Britain's grandest landowners, doing something not even my lawyer friends or my banker friends can afford to do."

What I'm saying here, in my convoluted, digressive, name-dropping way, is that the class system is and always has been a two-way street. Rich people don't just want to hang out with rich people. All rich people are really interested in is getting rich, being rich and staying rich, which is fine up to a point but not exactly conducive to deep thought or great conversation. So to make up for this lacuna in their affluent but culturally arid lives they like to surround themselves with one or two token wits, intellectuals, artists, actors, court jesters. It's a symbiotic relationship. Mr. and Mrs. Rich Person acquire the reflected glory of their glamorous arty friends. We scuzzy, rank-smelling court jesters get to drink the Cristal we could otherwise never afford. Everyone's a winner, but only if they choose to be.

Note please that "only if they choose to be." Like most right-wing libertarians, I'm a great believer in equality of opportunity. That is—in so far as it's possible without the ham-fisted agents of the state butting into our personal lives, wasting our money, and screwing things up—I think society works best when everyone feels they're getting a more or less even break.

The Left's version of this is communism or socialism, which I don't believe in at all. But nor do I believe in the state of affairs which exists in most of South America, where if you're not very, very rich you're exceedingly poor and probably stuck in the underclass forever. That way bloody revolution lies.

So what do I mean by this even break for everyone? Well I suppose the obvious example is equality before the law. No more should rich people be able to buy their way out of jail, than minorities should be able to do so by claiming oppressed victim status. I also believe that a smart kid from a poor background ought to be able to get as good an education—scholarships, maybe—as any rich person can buy. And that similar rules should apply to acting talents, musical prodigies, sporting geniuses, and so on. It's in everyone's interests that the cream should be allowed to rise to the surface, not only because it's through its elites—scientific, intellectual, and the top dogs in every other sphere—that a nation advances, but because of the escape route it offers to the indigent to transcend their lowly circumstances.

Unfortunately when Obama talks of equality I fear he means something entirely different. What he means by "equality" is the liberal-left version of "equality"—not equality of opportunity but equality of outcome. This state-enforced "fairness" is in fact the very opposite of fair because it completely overlooks the most fundamental point about human beings: we are all different.

Some of us are blessed with spectacularly attractive, curvy bodies we can make a career out of; some of us can do Difficult Sudoku puzzles in under five minutes; some of us can solve

Fermat's Last Theorem; some of us can smoke 100 cigarettes a day then die of old age; some of us don't sunburn easily; some of us can write snappy commercial jingles; some of us can throw a baseball a hundred miles an hour; some of us can pull trailers with our teeth; some of us can imitate the mating call of a curlew; some of us can handle poisonous snakes and never get bitten; some of us can charm worms; some of us are lucky; some of us have the gift of healing; some are particularly handy with a Barratt sniper rifle.

Is any of this fair? Of course it's not fair. But what are we going to do about it: poke out the eyes of all the sighted so blind people don't feel they're missing out? Enforce sex rationing for particularly attractive people so that they don't get any more nookie than the rest of us? Adopt a quota system for the New York Philharmonic whereby, for every piece it performs by a classically trained composer it has to play at least another by a tone-deaf amateur? (This more or less happens on French radio: for every decent British or American pop song they play they must, by order of the state, play some crappy French one. It's for the cultural good of the *La Republique*, don't you know.)

These may seem extreme examples but if you're going to punish rich people for being rich with swingeing taxes, why let all the other people with desirable attributes off the hook? Why not punish the beautiful and sweet-smelling for the unfair competitive advantage they have over the ugly and malodorous? Why not punish dope-smoking slackers for all that excess down time they enjoy? Why not handicap really good sportsmen and women by insisting they always play with one arm behind their backs? Why not force successful gamblers to pay half their winnings to losers?

You could go on micromanaging people's lives like this forever and still never achieve a totally "just" society. What would you do, say, about the people who lived longer than others? Enforce a *Logan's-Run*-style culling age? And what about Government?

How do you square the fact that out of all the 300 million Americans now living, no more than a handful will ever get to become president? Do you perhaps hand the job out on a rota basis whereby everyone gets to be president for fifteen minutes? Or would it be better to do it by lottery?

There are few social injustices in the world so unfair that they can't be made worse by well-intentioned government meddling. Consider once more those poor, overtaxed rich people. I'm not arguing that they shouldn't pay a proportion of their income to the state—how else are we going to have the wherewithal to feed our starving and nuke our enemies?—but I do question whether society will really benefit from making the pursuit of money a punishable offense. Making money, after all, often involves risk. It also often involves having no life whatsoever, multiple divorces, and an early grave. If for all this suffering, you don't even get keep the one thing that makes your grisly existence worthwhile, why go to all the bother? Why not just go and be a water-sports instructor on Bora Bora instead and spend your whole life in a South Pacific paradise rather than just the one miserable, Blackberry-dominated week over Thanksgiving?

Personally speaking, I rather enjoy living in a world so rife with inequality. It's what makes life interesting and varied. And it's what makes it such a thrilling challenge. So you're not quite as hunky and good-looking and athletic and co-ordinated as the sports jock with the locker next to you. But so what? Maybe you excel at some obscure sport he doesn't (Curling? Lacrosse? Tiddlywinks?); maybe he's as dense as the tax code, while you're a polished wit; or maybe you can do what Arnie did, and transform yourself from sand-kicked-in-the-face-on-the-beach guy into the Terminator.

I like the Arnie Schwarzenegger story. We all like the Arnie story because it gels so perfectly with one of our favorite primal myths: the ordinary guy (or girl) who, with a bit of hard work and a bit of luck, surprises all doubters, transcends his modest circumstances and proves to the world that he is, in fact, The One.

This is the basis for the popularity of the *Star Wars* franchise; for *The Matrix* trilogy; and of course for the multi-million dollar career of J. K. Rowling. We all want to be Luke Skywalker, Neo, and Harry Potter because, well hey, we all believe in our hearts we're kind of special—more special than anyone except maybe our mother quite appreciates—and that one day our time will come and we'll prove it to the world. It was certainly what was going through my own mind back in those Oxford university days when I used to fantasize about the letter in my pigeon-hole informing that I was about to become a Duke.

But here's the wonderful thing I've discovered about the world now that I'm so much older, so much more experienced, and so incredibly wise: life's what you make of it.

Yeah, I know. Suddenly, I'm sounding like Maya Angelou. Forrest Gump, even. I'm undermining my whole damned argument.

Wait, though. Hear me out, will you? And allow me one more cliché. It's my belief that social class isn't about where you're from but about where you're at. That we can be whoever we want to be. (Oops that's two clichés. Still with me, I hope. . . .)

I'm speaking from my own experience here, but I've no doubt you'll find moments in your life that tell the same story. I'm not a Duke's son. And I don't have an awful lot of money. Yet still, with a bit of ingenuity, I've been able to exploit those modest attributes I do possess in such a way as to get most of the things I ever wanted out of life.

So I don't own an estate. Yeah, but I've made enough of my career to find friends who've got one. So I can't afford expensive holidays. Yeah, but I'm a journalist and anywhere in the world I want to go I can get sent for free by a newspaper. So I was born into the boring middle class. Yeah, but by adjusting my accent and getting an Oxford education I've jumped at least half a social notch above my father. What's more, I now realize I actually quite enjoy being middle class.

The turning point was a conversation with my friend Alain de Botton (who annoyingly is much richer and more successful than me, but I can forgive him that because he's got much less hair). Alain, being Swiss, doesn't remotely understand the British class system, and was appalled when I confessed to him my upper class fantasy.

"But how could anything be more desirable than to be middle class?" Alain wanted to know. "The upper classes are just pampered layabouts. It's the middle classes that produce most of the things that make existence worthwhile. They write the great novels, they make the great paintings, they compose the great music.... " And of course, having aspirations in at least one of those departments myself, I am happy to accept that he is perfectly right.

No doubt if I'd been born into what in Britain we call the working class, I'd be very happy with that too. George Orwell once said that it is impossible for an Englishman to open his mouth without another Englishman despising him. This is quite true. Over here we are always forming judgements on one another based on tiny, seemingly trivial details like whether a person says "toilet" (rather than the socially smarter "loo") or how they pronounce the word "one." Don't pretend to me that something similar doesn't go in places like the Hamptons in August.

What makes our class system much less harsh than at first it seems, though, is that it is not merely a licence to despise your social inferiors and resent your social betters. It is also a way of making everyone feel better about themselves. Take the working classes. Technically speaking, they are the bottom of the social heap. Does this bother them? Does it hell! Talk to any working class person—if you can find one: almost everyone is middle class now—and their prevailing spirit will not be one of shame in being the underdog, but tremendous pride in being a horny-handed-son-of-toil, the engine-room of the economy, the source of all the world's rough-hewn wisdom, integrity, thrift, honesty and rugged good humor. Equality is the last thing any of them would want.

Equality is the last thing any of us should want. Not, at any rate, in Obama's sense of the word. We all have our own peculiar talents, we all have a way of getting what we want—if we want it enough—in the end. And if we don't want to play the game, if we want to just settle down and accept second best and enjoy an easier life, well that's our prerogative too in a free society. It's only when the state starts interfering in this natural, healthy process that the trouble starts. Not only does it unfairly skew the balance, rewarding those who've made no effort, punishing those who do, but it also demeans all aspiration and diminishes all achievement. After all, if you only got where you were because Big Government stepped in and did your work for you, how can you ever be truly satisfied?

Chapter Five

THINK THEY CAN'T BAN HUNTING?

I KNOW IN AMERICA YOU GO HUNTING with proper guns and take down deer and elk and caribou and turkeys and ducks and even bears. You have a proud hunting tradition, and you have powerful advocates for hunting and gun rights, like Ted Nugent and the NRA. President Obama would be foolish to try to deny you the Second Amendment rights guaranteed you by your Constitution. But he might try, at least at the margins. Since the Left doesn't trust you with your own money what makes you think they'll trust you with guns? As you know, in Britain, Canada, and Australia—the countries in the world most like yours—we've had to endure draconian gun bans, bans so stringent that our Olympic shooting team couldn't even practice in mainland Britain.

We still, however, retain a few ancient liberties yet, in socialist Britain, so it remains possible to go hunting with guns, at least to some extent, as per my foray into Scotland. But hunting in England has traditionally meant fox-hunting. In fact, England's rural heritage of fox-hunting is something most Americans associate with the old country.

Next time you come to England I'd like to take you out hunting. It'll cost you maybe five hundred bucks for the day (I'd pay myself, except I've spent twelve years living under a socialist tax regime), you won't be able to walk for a week afterwards, and there's a significant risk you'll end up paraplegic.

But hey, no pain, no gain, right? By the time dusk closes in and you kick your wearied nag homewards, you will have had more fun than you ever imagined possible whether clothed or unclothed, and with or without the help of booze, narcotics, tight breeches, whips, and small furry animals. More important, you will have learned what it means to be truly free.

You thought you knew this already? Well maybe. But fox hunting—or its possibly even more exciting cousin, stag-hunting—takes you to another realm altogether. It has the sexiest, most glamorous uniform this side of *Baywatch*: thick, high-buttoning coat like an eighteenth century gentleman's; butt-hugging jodhpurs; stock (tightly wound strip of white neckcloth designed partly to keep you warm, partly to hold your vertebrae intact when you fall off); leather boots; whip; nipple clamps; outsized codpiece.... (Oh all right the last two are optional).

It is—FACT—the world's only known sport (with the possible exception of darts) where your performance is actually improved by being drunk; nay, where sobriety is positively frowned upon for the deleterious effects it may have on your courage.

It is frequently associated with fornication, wife-swapping, stable-girl-rogering, fast-car-driving, and all manner of Rabelaisian excess, ribaldry, and licentiousness.

It demands courage, discipline, good humour, sang-froid, stamina, athleticism, skill, an understanding of nature and the landscape, a respect for hierarchy, a deep love of tradition and a frank and unapologetic acknowledgement of the atavistic killer instincts that lurk within us all, whatever the bleeding-heart tofu-munchers may claim.

Its primary aim is to chase photogenic, big-eyed, frequently anthropomorphized creatures (see for instance, *Bambi*; *The Fox and the Hound*) for miles and miles across open country, exhaust them, then shoot them, or let the hounds rip them to pieces, or both, before smearing their blood on your children's faces and pinning their heads or tails (the fox's or stag's, that is, not your children's) to your sitting room wall.

For some reason it irritates the hell out of the animal rights lobby.

Clearly, a sport with so many wonderful things going for it could never be allowed to survive under socialism. Which is why, of course, one of the British Labour government's first priorities on coming to power was to ban it.

You'll find out in a moment what became of that ban. (Clue: it failed, the British people's desire for liberty proving for once more powerful than their habit of obedience.) But first, let me describe for you some of the treats in store when you spend your first day "riding to hounds."

It'll still be dark when you wake and you won't want to get out of bed at all. The big old country house you'll be staying in— Georgian probably, with huge sash windows, none of them double-glazed—will be drafty and ill-heated. And the hunting season only starts when the wheat has been harvested—once the weather has started to get properly cold and miserable, in other words.

Shivering, you'll slip quickly into your unfamiliar kit, which includes a pair of women's tights—even if you're a man and only partly because of the British love of cross-dressing: it's mainly so as to keep your legs warm under your jodhpurs. When you reach the stock-tying stage you'll come and ask me for help. Sadly I don't know how to tie one either, so we'll have to wander round the long, echoing, carpetless corridors till we find someone who does. The stock, when it is completed, will feel unpleasantly tight, reminding you of the time in a previous life when you were hanged for pick-pocketing or garrotted by thuggee assassins in nineteenth century India. When you complain about this, the person who tied it will cheerily reply: "Ah but how else is your neck to stay together when you break it?"

You will hate this person for their good cheer when you personally are feeling so miserable, shivery, uncomfortable, and nervous. At breakfast, this hatred will intensify, for it will seem as if everyone at the long wooden table apart from you in the stone-flagged, dog-smelling kitchen is actually looking forward to this day of cold and uncertainty and wanton peril. Don't worry, it's just a ruse. What you're witnessing is no more than the sang-froid our mutual ancestors demonstrated as they squared up to one another for bloody slaughter at Lexington and Concord. Unfashionable, I know, in this age of sentiment, and panty-waistery, and wearing your heart on your sleeve. But hunting is the world that fashion forgot. Here people still remember how to do things properly.

This is why you'll have to eat your Full English breakfast, whether you like it or not. Greasy fried egg? Shrivelled black mushrooms? Fried tomato? Dodgy sausage made, no doubt, of ground pig's snout and pig's trotter and pig's God-knows-what else swept up into the mincer from the abbatoir floor? Black pudding made of chunks of pig fat suspended in foamy fried roundels of congealed pig's blood? It's not what your lurching stomach feels like, but down it you must—not just to show form, but also because you need your strength and you won't be eating again before sundown. Go easy on the coffee, though. It's not as though your nervous system needs any more geeing up. And the very last thing you need on horseback is a bursting bladder.

So you've forced your breakfast down somehow, and now you've been driven to the Meet, which is the place—normally the sweeping gravel driveway of some magnificent stately home—where the hunt gathers before it sets out. In a horsebox nearby, your mount awaits you. Because you're unfortunate enough not to own your own hunter (a type of sturdy horse bred specially for hunting; never used as a term for someone who hunts), you've had to pay 200 bucks or so for a "hireling." The stable-yard which has rented this horse to you has promised that it is an "honest" jumper (meaning it doesn't shy at fences) and that it is bomb-proof (meaning you're not going to die). You'll just have to take their word for it: it's too late to go looking for a replacement now.

Nervously, stiffly you clamber onto your mount. Apache he's called, which sounds kind of cute, till you remember the scalping and the hacking off of victims' eyelids in the pitiless New Mexico sun and that weird thing they used to do with their genitals, kind of sucking them up inside their body cavity before a battle so as not to get them chopped off. Whatever, Apache seems manageable enough. So he is, confides the sweet girl who has come along from the stable yard to monitor the various hirelings' progress. Just so long as you realize he's terrified of cows, runs a mile from tractors, tends to bite the tail of any horse that gets too close in front of him, jerks his head hard forward if you don't give him a loose enough rein, and gets very upset if he isn't at the front of the field so you must give him his head for he's far too strong to hold back. Apart from all that, though, he's a sweetheart.

By now you fully expect to die. In fact you feel so nauseated with fear you might almost be dead already. Your mind flits to the opening minutes of *Saving Private Ryan*, all those green-gilled, vomiting, shuddering GIs packed in their bucking, spray-soaked landing craft, half of them doomed to get drilled by the MG-42s in those Normandy cliffs before they've even hit the shore. "So THIS is what was going through those poor guys' heads? Jesus!"

Obviously you don't want to push that image too far. A day's fox-hunting or stag-hunting does not have nearly the same attrition rate or level of gut-churning horror as the American landings on Omaha Beach in June 6, 1944. But it is widely acknowledged, by those who've experienced both, to be the closest approximation to the adrenalized rush of combat you can get outside the military. That's why the Duke of Wellington—George Washington too, I shouldn't wonder—preferred all his young officers to be fox-hunting men. And why among the most distinguished British armored units in the Second World War—such as the Sherwood Rangers—were county yeomanry regiments led by impetuous young officers who'd cut their teeth in the hunting field.

This is where the hooch comes in handy. You're not going to feel seriously better till you've had your first gallop, which tends to dispel all those pent-up nerves. Till then, you're best off having a drink. Several drinks in fact. So you grab one of the glasses from the trays being handed round the hunt's supporters. Then another. And another. And suddenly you begin to see this whole crazy, suicide circus in a completely different light.

You notice the extraordinary old world courtesy—the way all the men tip their riding hats when first greeting a lady; the way everyone rides up to bid a polite "good morning" to the red-coated Master (who is in charge of the hunt), and the Field Master (who is in charge of the Field—that is, you and all the other riders who are following the hunt on horseback); the way nervous newcomers—you, again—are quickly welcomed into the fold and introduced round.

You also notice how overpoweringly sexy it all is: the pert buttocks, the firm, muscular legs astride rippling, gleaming horse flesh; the russet-cheeked girls and ripe, middle-aged farmer's wives with their riding crops, their hair severely bunched in nets, their expressions determined and set like something from your favourite dominatrix fantasy; the men all virile and immaculate like Jane Austen heroes; the suggestive thrusting motion of the rising trot; the scent of leather and horse. This isn't just a sport, you realize. It's a sublimated orgy.

Before you've got time to get too carried away with all this excitement, though, the moment you've at once longed for and dreaded arrives: after a quick speech from the Master, the hunt sets off in pursuit of its quarry, with the field—that's you and all the other riders following the hunt, remember—keeping up as best it can. You think: "Whoa! Wait a minute! Where's everybody going? I'm not ready for this."

Ready or not, the hunt has a job to do. What a lot of people don't realize about hunting is that most of the riders are just mounted spectators. The hunt itself is the tiny group comprising the Master, the huntsman (dressed in red—or "pink" as its called in hunting circles, even though it's not—so he can be more easily spotted by the Field), his two or three assistants (known as Whippers-In), and his pack (the thirty or so hounds—never dogs—with bloodlines often extending back centuries, every one of them known to the Huntsman by name). It is this group's task to follow the fox's scent, chase the fox out of its favorite woodland hidey-holes (known as "drawing covert"), pursue it across country and then—so long as it doesn't elude the hounds—kill it, usually with a single bite to its neck by the lead hound. Everyone else's job is keep back a reasonable distance and let hounds get on with their task unencumbered.

Not that you'll understand much of this on your first day's hunting. You won't understand the meaning of the huntsman's bizarre ululations (some of them dating from the Middle Ages), or the notes he sounds on his horn, or the arcane terminology (hounds "speak," they don't bark; they have "sterns" instead of rears), or the terrifying, unbreachable taboos like the one which dictates that under no circumstances are you ever allowed to over-take the field master. If you breach the etiquette, you get shouted at, and hunting people—especially the dragon-like grand dames—can be very fierce.

But it won't matter one bit because you'll be having the time of your life. As will your mount. Horses are herd animals, never happier than when surging forward en masse, feeding off one another's excitement and just generally hanging out with their own kind. If you like riding but have only ever done so alone, or in a small group, you haven't really been riding at all. Hunting is the real thing. The ONLY thing, most hunting folk would probably tell you. And once you've tried it, you'll feel towards those who haven't rather as new parents feel towards the childless: kind of sorry for them that they've missed out on the true purpose of existence.

No really, it's that good. You know how Korean War Sabre pilots can still remember every last detail of every dogfight they fought in the early 1950s with Chinese and Russian MiG pilots, every corkscrew, every roll, every dive from first encounter to final kill? Well that's just how it is with hunting. The terror, the exhilaration, the level of concentration and awareness and effort required just to stay on your horse, the way everything seems to come at you all at once in one massive impressionistic rush—the intensity is such that every moment is seared permanently in your brain.

Like an LSD trip, I remember thinking that first time I rode to hounds amid the psychotropic splendour of Exmoor in Devon with its precipitous valleys, chuckling streams, wooded slopes, bogs, and wild, windswept uplands like something the Dark Riders might pursue you across in *Lord of the Rings*. Like LSD, only better, because it's real and the flashbacks you get are (mostly) good flashbacks: the whooping joy when thirty or more of you gallop in line abreast—like in a cavalry charge—across open moor; the electric shock of terror you feel as the horse immediately in front trips in a rabbit hole and unseats its rider, mingled with gratitude that it isn't you and apprehension that it might yet happen to you, giving way to cheery stoicism that if it does happen to you it'll happen very quickly and there's nothing you can do about it, so what's the use of worrying? Just go with the flow.

You'd think there'd be no room for any of that hippy shit in a pursuit as raw and bloody and reactionary as hunting. Quite the opposite is true, though, I'd say. All those Emersonian tree-huggers and Enviro-crazy Ben-and-Jerry-munchers and anti-nuclear vegans with plaited hair bristling from their unshaven armpits, all those Al Gore fans and PETA types who imagine the world would be the most perfect place if only we bombed ourselves back to the Stone Age, lived in yurts, restored the barter system and connected with nature as only man can in his pure, unsullied primeval state. I'd say they're chasing exactly the same rural idyll hunting people are, only in a clumsier more self-loathing way.

Take their love of animals. The bunny huggers think they have a monopoly on this, but theirs is a shallow, warped, self-indulgent kind of love based on the mawkish notion that animals are just like us, pretty much, only nicer because they didn't invent Abu Ghraib or the atom bomb. Hunting people can't afford such sentiment, but that doesn't mean they hate animals. In fact they probably love them more deeply than anyone. To hunt an animal you must first understand it and respect it. To ensure that there are more of its kind to hunt in the future, you must learn how to nurture it and preserve its habitat. It's hunting people, not the greens, who wrote the book on conservation.

And have you ever tried spending five or more hours in the saddle on a horse so crazed with adrenalin that you're barely in control, knowing—as your horse does too, on some level—that the slightest mistake by either one of you could be the sudden death of both of you? You're in this one together, *homo sapiens* and

equus caballus—in it together through the good times and the
bad, the stirring gallops, the flying leaps, the skiddy, scary, down-
hill-in-the-thick-mud bits, the bogs, and the rain. It's an extraordinary bonding process. Never will you feel so connected with the
animal kingdom as you do when out hunting; never so at one with
the landscape. You, your horse, the other riders, the other horses,
the hounds and your quarry—the fox or the deer—are bound
together in this ancient ritual of the chase, the same one your
ancestors have been practising since mankind first learned to wield
a club or throw a spear.

In Britain, fox-hunting only really took off as a sport in the
eighteenth century, after the previous most popular quarry—
deer—had started to run out. (All right; so hunters don't always
get the conservation bit right). Admire the English countryside
today and what you are applauding is not nature but the careful
handiwork of gentleman landowners who have fashioned it for
their sporting interests: picturesque stone walls and verdant
cropped hedges rather than cheaper, uglier barbed wire fences
because walls and hedges are much nicer to jump on a horse;
woods, copses, and areas of scrub to enable foxes to hide in and
game birds to breed in. So chalk that one up too to the hunting
fraternity: they've helped improve on nature. Anti-hunting types
would hate to admit this. In their bitter, self-hating view, man can
only be a blot on the landscape, never its savior.

There's another thing about hunting the hippies would dig, if
only they could learn to suspend their prejudice. That's the camaraderie. Maybe they wouldn't so much identify with the wartime
brothers-in-arms aspect of this camaraderie—the you-watch-my-
back-I'll-watch-yours fellow feeling which comes from shared discomfort, excitement, and danger. But I'll bet they'd have no
problems with the other part of it: the one that resembles the
loved-up beneficence you get at an Ecstasy-fuelled rave.

That drugs thing again. I know. It's true all the same, when you're sharing some fevered pitch of heightened emotion, a prolonged adrenaline rush and you catch the eyes of all the other people you're sharing it with and say: "Yeah! Aren't we lucky? Isn't this amazing? Isn't this just the best time ever?" Well that's exactly how it is during the hunt.

Not when you're galloping, obviously. There's no time to exchange cute little glances when there's a dozen of you funnelling at full pelt towards a five-foot jump that you can only take one at a time. But there are lots of moments where you're just hanging around, freezing your ass off, waiting for something to happen, with this random group of people you've never met before but who in the next five minutes will become your bosomest buddies.

What might just take you aback as you hang out is what a socially mixed bunch they are. Fox-hunting has a reputation as a sport for the rich and privileged—the Prince of Wales was a big enthusiast up until the ban; many hunts are named after and still sometimes headed by Dukes and Earls—but you are as likely to find yourself riding alongside farm laborers and nurses and other salt-of-the-earth working types as you are with bowler-hatted grandees. There'll be six-year-olds on fat ponies, middle-aged housewives, ninety-year-olds who've been hunting since before the war. All ages are here; all classes; bound together by their love of a common cause.

Someone will pass you a drink, just like they do with plastic water bottles at a rave, only this one comes in a silver flask and contains cherry brandy, sloe gin, or kummel, because you can never have too much Dutch courage in a sport as dangerous as hunting. And you'll all exchange those complicitous grins that say: "God I feel sorry for all the people in the world who aren't here with us doing what we're doing right now."

But wait just a minute: if hunting with hounds has been made officially illegal, how come it is still carrying on as normal? That's the weird thing: it is, and it isn't. On the one hand, very few hunts have been forced to close—in England and Wales at least; the socialists were much more successful in Scotland—and their membership lists, post-ban have increased by as much as 40 percent thanks to hunting's new image as something exciting and naughty. On the other hand though, a conviction for hunting with hounds can land you a large fine or a prison sentence. Which is why every hunt has been forced to find loopholes in the law.

Most get round the problem by pretending that they are drag hunting—pursuing a previously laid scent over a cross-country trail rather than a real live animal. Some bring along a bird of prey, it still being legal to flush out a fox using, say, a falcon and then shoot it. But this is mainly for the benefit of any police who may be watching, or any Antis (animal rights protestors and hunt saboteurs) who might be filming with video cameras to try to secure a prosecution. Once safely out of view, the hunting goes on as before. Hunt masters understand that in order to convict them, a court must first prove beyond reasonable doubt that they "intended" to hunt the fox with their hounds. But suppose that while following a legal drag trail their hounds—oops—accidentally chanced upon the scent of a real fox, gave chase and killed it; well hey, hounds will be hounds and what can a poor huntsman do to stop them?

And why, given that there are so many more pressing issues out there, did the British Labour government devote such effort trying to railroad through this unpopular, unenforceable ban in the first place? Well I guess it might not have been unconnected with the million pound, strings-attached donation the Labour party was given by a U.S. animal rights organization PAL (Political Animal Lobby). It also, I'm sure, had to do with class hatred; metropolitan politicians' fear and incomprehension of their rural minority; and, yes, the fashionable PC notion that foxes and stags have feelings too.

Mainly though, it was because hunting represents such a spectacular affront to so many of the liberal left's most cherished sacred cows. Being rooted in tradition, history, and primitive, atavistic bloodlust it offends the Left's belief in social progress and the perfectibility of human nature. Being tremendously enjoyable it offends the Left's puritanical fear of pleasure. Being popular, effective, well-run, and entirely self-financing, it offends the Left's belief that only the state truly understands how to make things work. Being closer and more sympathetic to nature than most eco-warriors and animal rights activists could hope to be in a million years, it offends the Left's belief that only it truly understands the environment.

You think the hunting debate is about something as trivial as animal rights? Yeah, we used to think that way too. But it's not. It goes much deeper than that, to the very essence of the philosophical battle between left and right. Who best understands how you ought to behave: yourself or your Government? I know which way I'm voting. With the good guys. With the hunters.

Chapter Six

BARBECUE THE POLAR BEARS

THE MOST TERRIFYING SPEECH I've heard your new socialist president utter so far—mind you, it's early days; give him time—is the one on the video shown in December 2008 to delegates at a UN climate change conference in Poland. It went something like:

"...And furthermore, though the wrinkly little green guy got home THIS time, I want to be sure that he gets home EVERY time. To this end, it is the intention of my administration to invest $200 billion in a new Extraterrestrial Communications Program, to ensure that whenever future stranded ETs phone home, they'll get through to Mom straight away.

"Now, I'd like to talk about my plans to combat the current most dangerous threat facing all humanity. I refer, of course, to Lord Voldemort and his plans to enslave not just the wizarding world but the Muggle one too. There are those such as my predecessor who claim that 'He-Who-Must-Not-Be-Named,' as some call him, does not exist. I however—having seen the movie and believed every word—know better. It is consequently my intention to impose a 20 percent levy on all business to finance a new $1 trillion Department of Magic with its own secretary (David Copperfield) and under-secretary (David Blaine) and sweeping powers to do whatever it sees fit under whichever circumstances to whomsoever it chooses till the end of time."

If he had said any of this, you'd be a bit worried, wouldn't you? But not half as worried as you ought to be by what he actually said, which was all about America's new role in the fight to "save the planet" from global warming.

"The science is beyond dispute and the facts are clear," he said. "Sea levels are rising, coastlines are shrinking, we've seen record drought, spreading famine and storms that are growing stronger with each passing hurricane season."

Few of these statements have any factual basis.

Your new president has gone to the movies. Seen one he particularly likes by a guy named Al. And without bothering to do any background reading, has transformed this guy Al's weird fantasy into official, eye-wateringly expensive U.S. government policy.

Yeah, exactly. That loser presidential candidate you thought you'd escaped forever has snuck in the back door and is gearing up to charge you the earth to "save" the earth. And this time it will take more than a few dimpled chads to stop him.

One thing you can definitely expect to see under the new Gorebama presidency is the entrenchment of self-righteous eco-fascism. The environmental terror—global warming, as it is now, or the threat of a new ice age (which was fashionable a few decades earlier), or whatever they decide the problem is—obviously requires all sorts of government controls, initiatives, and busybody interference in your life.

And it will all be dressed up as our duty to the planet—or to the true believers, as our duty to Gaia, the new earth goddess deity of the Left—not to mention to all those cute polar bears sadly on the verge of extinction…except they're not. Have you noticed that they never mention that polar bears are man-killers? Women and cute girls too—they don't discriminate that way.

I know because I've gone to Svalbard in Norway to meet the vanishing polar bears. Sadly I was too late. Every one of them had disappeared. Melted by global warming!

That's what I tell all my friends when they ask how my trip was. It's much more of a fun answer than the truth which is: "We went to the wrong bit of the island, where there aren't so many bears. They're much harder to spot than you'd think: only one in ten visitors to Svalbard gets to see them. We were only there three days. Should have gone to Churchill, Manitoba, where they're commoner than pigeons in Time Square." Also, I never like to miss a chance to mock the Great Endangered Polar Bear Myth. We're all in danger of taking it far, far, FAR too seriously.

Don't get me wrong. I'd love to see a polar bear in the wild, I really would. I like the fact that they're all fluffy and white (well, actually, they're more of a dirty yellow but let's skip over that one) and photogenic. What I like even more is that they're so darned dangerous.

Soon as you get to the airport at Longyearbyen (that's the capitol of the most populous island on the Svalbard peninsula, named after the Bostonian coal miner who founded it, John Munroe Longyear), you start seeing tantalising signs warning of the POLAR BEAR DANGER.

Not so long ago, two girls went hiking up the mountain just the other side of the fjord from Longyearbyen. Only one of them came back. The other had been savagely chomped by a polar bear—the world's largest land predator and one of the few animals on earth known actively to hunt and kill humans. That's why on Svalbard, you're not allowed to go a few yards outside the main settlements unless you're carrying a gun.

Dangerous animals are cool. But you SO wouldn't want to be eaten by one. I think of the USS *Indianapolis* and all those torpedoed sailors floating in the Pacific for three days, slowly being picked off by the sharks: Tigers, and Oceanic Whitetips. I think of the thousand Japanese soldiers—the world's worst-ever animal related atrocity—gobbled up by Saltwater crocodiles during the battle of Ramree Island in 1945. And I've never been able to watch *Frasier* or Sideshow Bob on *The Simpsons* in quite the same way since I learned that poor Kelsey Grammer's half-brothers were both eaten by sharks.

I used to think it was my destiny to be eaten by one too. I once wrote an autobiographical novel about it, called *Fin*, in which I included all my favorite true shark-death-horror stories, and to give it a good ending I thought I'd have a scene where the hero goes down in a cage to confront his ultimate fear.

For added verisimilitude, I did this myself in South Africa at a place called Shark Alley which—as its name subtly hints—contains perhaps the densest concentration of great white sharks anywhere in the world. And do you know what? It wasn't scary because it just didn't seem real. I'd watched so many shark documentaries on the Discovery Channel that seeing two genuine great whites swimming just inches away from me felt routine almost to the point of dullness. Also, having watched great whites in action over several days I learned something you don't really get out of books or TV: they're not really these dumb voracious predators which will snap at anything be it a seal, a surfboard, or a human. Sure they do do those things now and then. But on the whole they're quite intelligent and cautious. If I'd fallen off the side of that boat while the sharks were circling, I really don't reckon they would have gone for me. I'm sorry to say the experience rather killed my fear of sharks.

Back to the polar bears. The reason I've gone to Svalbard, looking for them, is because I'm on a publicity junket with a team of wildlife documentary makers from the BBC. They've made this fabulously beautiful nature movie called *Earth*—perhaps you saw it? the one where the polar bear mother and her cubs emerge from their snow hole for the first time, and the babies slide cutely down the slope—and I've got to write a color piece about how great it is, how stunning Svalbard is, how difficult and dangerous polar bears are to film, etc.

Beats working for a living. We get to stay at the world's northernmost fully serviced hotel—the SAS Radisson Polar Hotel; we visit amazing weird places like the grim old Russian mining town where there are busts of Lenin and it's like travelling back in time to the Soviet Union; best of all, we get to ride 300 miles across stunning arctic landscapes on skidoos. Thank God the BBC's paying for all this. Do you know how much a beer costs at Oslo airport? Sixteen bucks, that's how much. Seriously, don't ever, ever go to Norway unless it's on a business trip.

So there are maybe ten other journalists on this trip from all around the world—the earnest Germans, the Japanese guys with all the cameras, and so on—all making the right, concerned eco-noises about the polar bear's plight, man's guilt, the melting ice caps, and the need for urgent carbon emissions reductions. And there am I feeling a bit like the spy in *Where Eagles Dare*. Everyone else thinks I'm one of them, that I'm on side, that I share the same mission aims. But I'm not—I'm the traitor, the one who doesn't believe remotely in their idiotic cause, the one they're going to have to kill. Best to keep my feelings to myself, then.

"Don't mention the environment. Just don't!" my wife is forever telling me. Quite rightly, too, for whenever I do it almost always gets me into trouble. Living in London, as I do, you're totally surrounded by smug, sanctimonious, bourgeois eco-zealots who pootle around in electric cars, recycle like it's the new religion (which it is), only eat organic, and actually boast about how incredibly complicated and arduous their three day journey by train, bus, and rickshaw to Tuscany was this year because they want you to know how good they feel about not having used an evil, carbon-unfriendly airplane.

These are not the kind of people you want to get into an argument with about climate change. Not because they know more stuff than you—they mostly don't—but because in their eyes anyone who even thinks to countenance the possibility that global warming isn't happening and that it isn't all man's fault is anathema, a heretic, beyond the pale of all decency and reason. "Climate-change denial," that's what the swivel-eyed eco-loon George Monbiot calls it. And he believes it ought to be made a crime on a par with Holocaust Denial.

Come again? You're seriously trying to tell us, George, that a man who despite all the evidence of Auschwitz, Sobibor, and Treblinka claims that six million Jews were never murdered by Hitler deserves the same contempt as a guy who has watched *An Inconvenient Truth* and decided that on balance it's a pile of crap? Puh-lease. And I thought it was us climate-change deniers who were supposed to be the crazy ones.

Blimey, though, that Al Gore movie has a lot to answer for. (Incidentally, before we're done with the Holocaust, I was ashamed to notice that one of the people who lost out on the Nobel Peace prize the year Gore and the Intergovernmental Panel on Climate Change won it was a brave woman who had risked her life to save dozens of Jews from the Nazis.) Naturally I went along to the cinema to find what the fuss was about and two things immediately struck me. One, what a genius huckster Gore must be to persuade millions of people that a creaky film of a dull power point lecture by a failed presidential candidate was in fact the most urgent, compelling, and important movie in history. (Truly, not since Leni Riefenstahl's *Triumph of the Will* has there been such a brilliantly successful propaganda exercise.) Two, how tongue-lollingly, slaveringly desperate the kids in the audience were to be told how guilty and wrong mankind is.

You could scarcely hear the soundtrack for all the eager grunting, vigorous head-nodding "uh-huhs," and consensual sighing coming from the auditorium. "Yes, yes, OH YES, UNCLE AL!" my neighbours all seemed to be saying. "Tell us how bad we have been. That bad? REALLY THAT BAD? We've been naughty, Uncle Al. We know we've been naughty. Now you must tell us how we should be punished. What's that you say, Uncle Al? Hair shirts? Yes, that's good. Very good. We like wearing hair shirts. And you're saying also we should abandon all the luxuries man has acquired in 5,000 years of civilization? Mmm. Do it to us, babyyyyy.... "

The true brilliance of *An Inconvenient Truth*, I think, lay in its timing. It came out when growing public disaffection with George W. Bush was prompting more and more people to think starry-eyed thoughts of what might have been, if only poor, nice Al's victory had not been so cruelly snatched by those dimpled chads. More important, it coincided with the peak of one of the greatest economic booms in history, when people were just beginning to ask themselves: "Hmm. Have we maybe had it too good for a little too long? Oughtn't we to be punished for all this decadence?"

Mankind has always had this self-flagellatory instinct, this idea that periods of bounty can never be enjoyed without paying some terrible cosmic price. It's what drove our early ancestors to propitiate the gods by sacrificing their most desirable virgins; it's what drove some penitents in the Middle Ages to whip themselves and spend a fortune buying "indulgences" for their sins, thus diminishing the time they would spend in Purgatory before ascending to Heaven.

That's what carbon trading and carbon offsetting are: the twenty-first century equivalent of medieval indulgences. You pay your money to some ludicrous charlatan outfit which promises that by planting six mango trees they can magically carbon-neutralize the environmental costs of your flight from Washington, D.C., to Heathrow. *Et voila*: your conscience is salved and the world is saved!

Global warming is the latest fashionable variation on original sin. Now that so many fewer people, in the West at any rate, take traditional religion seriously they need to find themselves a secular replacement. Environmentalism fits the bill just perfectly, because it has most of the key ingredients the Religions of the Book do: the guilt, the sense that only through suffering can there be redemption, and the blind, unswerving faith in the pronouncements of a higher power. (Variously God; Jesus; Mohammed; Gore).

As during any period of widespread religious dogma, it simply doesn't do to rock the boat. You might indeed know better than your credulous contemporaries, but as in Stalin's Russia (Marxism being another modern, secular alternative to the Religions of the Book), which is more sensible: to keep schtum and have a quiet life? Or speak the truth and risk being put on a show trial? And why argue anyway with people who aren't interested in arguing? As far they're concerned the case is closed.

This is the key point Al Gore wants to get across in *An Inconvenient Truth*: the debate is over; all the scientists are in agreement; only a few nutcases on the extreme fringe now question the "Truth" that global warming is dangerous, man-made, and can only be averted if we destroy our economy and relive the Dark Ages. Thus does the authentic voice of liberalism seek to silence every one of the thousands of courageous scientists, analysts, researchers, and statisticians out there who continue to refute these claims and are prepared to stake their careers on it. Damn near gets away with it too.

It's scarcely the first time the liberal-left has used this technique to silence its opponents. It's a method known as "Closing Down the Argument" and it's the last refuge of a scoundrelous ideology which knows that whenever it's exposed to the cut and thrust of rational debate, it rarely comes out the winner. This is something the great Rush Limbaugh noticed long ago. "The Right," he said, "is always going to win the intellectual argument; the Left is always going to win the emotional one." Hence the liberal left's ongoing reluctance to deal with anything that smells like fact, hard evidence, or close detailed analysis.

Here in Britain, certainly, this method has allowed the Left to get away with murder. Question, for example, the growing power of the socialist European super-state and you are dismissed as a "Little Englander" or a xenophobe; quibble about unchecked immigration and you are racist; worried about the growing prevalence of veils on Muslim girls in schools and you are an Islamophobe; suspect that the eco-lobby is overstating its case and you are a "Climate Change Denier." You've seen similar tricks played in America over issues like Nuclear Power. Instead of being allowed to engage in free debate about its viability, every nuance of your argument is rejected in just three words: Three Mile Island. Or maybe even two: China Syndrome.

Note that in all the above cases, the liberal left is taking great care to avoid a pitched battle on your home turf. Like the Viet Cong, like the Taliban, like al Qaeda in Iraq, it wants to grind you down, bide its time, go for the weak points. Rather than attack the near impregnable logic of your position, it tries to undermine it by sneering at your motives. The reason you believe in low taxes is because you're mean and selfish. The reason you don't believe in global warming is either because you're too lazy to mend your planet-destroying ways or you just like being controversial.

A journalist friend of mine tried this the other day when he went to interview Rush Limbaugh. The only bit that really shocked him, he wrote, were Limbaugh's views on global warming which (my friend claimed) contradicted the views of

98 percent of the world's scientists. Had Limbaugh deliberately adopted this stance, he wondered, just to be provocative?

This says more about the Greens' complacency than it does about Limbaugh. So rarely do they hear their position challenged—as much as anything because they're not interested in listening—it simply never occurs to them that there might be doubts about its viability. It's why, when you do challenge their Inconvenient Truth with a few inconvenient truths of your own, their reaction tends to veer between outrage and shrill disbelief.

Just recently I went to interview a guy who runs a highly successful art-cum-eco project (heavily subsidized by all the usual worthy, left-leaning funding bodies) which involves travelling with various groovy writers, painters, sculptors, video-installationists, and musicians up to the Arctic Circle in a beautiful old sailing boat. They get to travel for free and enjoy the trip of a lifetime. The deal is that in return, they eventually make an art-work that spreads the word about the threat of global warming.

"Hey, nice job!" I said. And meant it because the High Arctic's a beautiful place and what could be cooler than to be paid by charitable foundations to hang out there with talented, clever, famous people? "It's not about me. It's about saving the planet," he replied priggishly. Because I didn't want to jeopardize the interview, I held my true feelings over till the end. (My wife, yet again, had strictly ordered me not to bring them up. But hey, I'm a man and this guy's eco-righteousness had got my tail up.) "Do you know how much global mean temperatures have risen in the last thirteen years?" I asked.

"Yes," he said. "0.7 degrees."

Not long after that, he started getting really quite cross, professing astonishment that I, a mere journalist, thought I knew better than all the world's scientific experts, accusing me of being a wanton controversialist, and of not knowing my facts. The last accusation I found particularly interesting because of his answer to my first question.

Global temperatures haven't risen at all in the last thirteen years. For ten years they remained level and in the last three they have been dropping. So we're currently in a period of global cooling. But our friend didn't want to know. (That 0.7 degrees figure, incidentally, is the global temperature increase, in Centigrade, for the whole of the twentieth century. Yikes! A bit more than half of one degree. Doesn't that make you feel SO threatened?)

You might reasonably wonder how it can be that a man who has chosen to dedicate his career to a particular cause should yet be ignorant of the facts surrounding its most important underlying principle. I don't wonder at all. It's of a piece with almost every argument I've had on the subject of climate change with the Greens. The sincerity of their passion and the intensity of their love for the planet, they believe, trumps everything.

As something of a planet lover myself I find this arrogance rather irritating. When I watch sea otters frolicking amid the kelp on the coast of Northern California, I don't find myself thinking: what those critters need is a really big oil slick. When I watch plastic bags accumulating in thorn trees in the remote desert wastes of Djibouti, I don't go: hurrah! Civilization comes to Africa at last! When I read that the snowy crest of Kilimanjaro (which I once summited as a teenager—almost: I got altitude sickness) will soon be no more, I don't go: huh, that'll teach you, Papa Hemingway!

I like nature. I think most of us do. Even Wall Street bankers and tax collectors. Even oil men. We all recognize that clean sea is nicer to swim in than polluted sea; that beaches are much more pleasant when free of used condoms and syringes; that trees are the planet's lungs; that lots of fish is better than hardly any fish; all that nice, the planet-is-our-friend stuff we learn in the early years at school—we haven't forgotten it and we've since seen it for ourselves.

Yet you'd never guess this from the way Green campaigners carry on. Listen to Greenpeace. Listen to Al Gore. They present the world as a Manichean divide between the saintly environmentalists whose only interest is to preserve the planet, and evil, Gaia-raping-scum who want to destroy it utterly. In the latter camp, of course, they include anyone who disagrees with them about global warming. The message has been widely bought. It's a propaganda coup which does much to explain why so many are so reluctant to confront the reigning Green orthodoxy.

Consider the fate of Danish statistician Bjørn Lomborg. In global-warming-denial terms he's a pretty low grade offender: he professes concern about anthropogenic global warming, finds himself in broad agreement with the International Panel on Climate Change, but just happens to think there are better ways to spend money than on a harebrained agreement—the Kyoto Protocol—which, at an annual cost to the world economy of $150 billion would postpone the effects of global warming by just six years.

He first made these claims in his influential book *The Skeptical Environmentalist* and has been vilified for it ever since. He has been called the "Antichrist," attacked by numerous scientific journals, denounced as "unscientific" by a semi-official group called The Danish Committees on Scientific Dishonesty, and had a custard pie thrown in his face by an eco-campaigner at a British book signing.

One of the things the Greens hate most about Lomborg is that he is an apostate. A left-leaning Greenpeace member, he had set himself and his university students the task of disproving shocking claims by a right-wing American scientist that the global eco-system wasn't really in so terrible a state as the mung-bean-munchers and tree-huggers usually claimed. To his horror, he found the right-winger's arguments were correct, and set out to demonstrate this in a book which made full use of exactly the same statistics that organizations such as Greenpeace and the World Wildlife Fund were using to whip up eco-hysteria.

This was Lomborg's second major crime. He uttered truths which, for the Guardians of the Eternal Flame of Global Eco-Righteousness, ought forever to have remained hidden. My personal favorite was the stuff the plucky blond Dane came up with about the Exxon Valdez disaster. Remember how bad the news stories encouraged us to feel about what was, after all, one of the world's top twenty worst oil spills—266,000 barrels of the stuff washed up in pristine Prince William Sound, Alaska? Well Lomborg's insights don't make exactly cozy reading for the bleeding hearts.

He reveals, for example, that the 260,000 sea birds killed by the disaster, tragic though this was, is no greater than the number of birds killed in the United States in a single day while flying into plate glass windows; nor than the number of birds killed every two days in Britain by domestic cats. The price of that clean up was $2 billion, which we'd all surely consider money well spent. Until, perhaps, we learn from Lomborg the fact that the beaches which had been expensively cleaned and pressure-washed took between eighteen months and two and half years longer to recover than those polluted beaches which (by way of a control in the experiment) had been left untouched.

Truth has often proved something of an inconvenience for the global eco movement. Perhaps it's because its adherents believe, like Winston Churchill during the war, that their particular version of the truth is so precious it "should always be attended by a bodyguard of lies." This would chime with the admission by NASA scientist James Hansen—with Al Gore, the arch high priest of the global warming religion—that "emphasis on extreme scenarios" may once have been "appropriate" among scientists trying to raise public awareness of the global warming threat.

Sound vaguely familiar? It should because it's the same phenomenon I mentioned earlier in my chapter on how the Left
ruined my sex life. Just as our governments did back in the Eighties in their misrepresentation of the AIDS threat, so scientists are
doing now with the supposed global warming threat. They have
decided if ever Joe Public gets to be apprised of all the facts, he
might draw the *wrong* conclusion, and that therefore he should
only be fed those bits of information which will help him reach
the *right* conclusion.

Karl Marx would surely have approved, for this is what he
meant when he talked about "false consciousness." This was his
notion that the ordinary people—that's you and I—have been so
corrupted by the reigning bourgeois-capitalist hegemony that they
cannot possibly be trusted to know what is good for them. Higher
agencies—Big Government; Big Al Gore—must consequently
make their decisions for them instead.

What depresses me hugely as a professional journalist is how
complicit our media have been in spreading the Great Global
Warming Myth. Where's the investigative spirit of Watergate, I'd
like to know? Or are conspiracies only worth investigating when
they're evil right-wing conspiracies? Are there conspiracies so
unquestionably noble in their intentions that the only thing a good
journalist can do is disseminate them as widely as possible?

That's certainly the impression I get from the newspapers. Sure
there are honourable exceptions—even more so in the Blogos-
phere. But on my side of the Atlantic and on yours, the vast
majority of the articles written about the environment tend to
come from the warmist, eco-hysterical perspective.

Sure bad news sells better than good news, but I think it runs
deeper than that. It has to do with the way so many of these stories are now written by specialist environmental correspondents.
And the sort of person predisposed to become an environmental
correspondent, is going to be predisposed to the idea that Mother

Nature is in peril and it's All Our Fault. The fact that they then get so much of their information from *parti pris* organizations like the Sierra Club, the National Resources Defense Council, the Union of Concerned Scientists, and the World Wildlife Fund—none of which exactly has an interest in talking the problem down—scarcely results in sterling objectivity.

This would explain why so many of the "facts" we know about global warming aren't really facts at all. The one I mentioned earlier about the disappearing snows on Kilimanjaro. It makes a great before and after photo, for sure. One which goes nicely with all the other ones showing how dramatically the world's glaciers have retreated. But it has no relevance whatsoever to global warming. By far the most extensive melting took place as long ago as 1912 and 1913. And besides, it has since been proved to have been caused by locals chopping down too many trees for firewood. Problem for the warmists is, blaming African natives isn't nearly so useful as blaming guilty white men.

And what about the famous "Hockey Stick Curve," the graph purporting to show how after centuries of stable termperatures, the second half of the twentieth century saw an exponential rise in global temperatures caused by man's carbon emissions? This is the one Al Gore exploited for hilarious comic effect in his movie when he had to climb a step ladder in order to demonstrate—cue much gasping from his audience—*just how high* that those terrifying, we're-going-to-fry temperatures would soon be going. Except they won't. The Hockey Stick Curve has since been widely demonstrated by scientists and statisticians to be unreliable to the point of uselessness. (For the full story on that, read Tom Bethell's *The Politically Incorrect Guide to Science* and Christopher C. Horner's *The Politically Incorrect Guide to Global Warming and the Environment,* two books the fanatics don't want you to read.)

But like the Arnie's evil cyborg at the end of *The Terminator,* that Hockey Stick Curve just keeps on coming. The Greens refuse to let it die. They like their Hockey Stick. It's iconic. It's dramatic. Their audience can relate to it. Just one look at that graph and you understand everything: we're in trouble; BIG TROUBLE; So much trouble that NO MEASURE IS TOO EXTREME, TOO EXPENSIVE to confront this, THE GREATEST THREAT THE WORLD HAS EVER KNOWN.

Never let the facts get in the way of a good story, right? Or as the newspaper editor puts it in *The Man Who Shot Liberty Valance*, "When the legend becomes fact, print the legend." Problem is, it isn't a movie we're talking about here. This is real life, our life, and if these sexy lies are allowed to continue unchecked they're going to be the ruination of us all.

Consider the U.S. Supreme Court's ruling that the U.S. Environmental Protection Agency should treat CO_2 as a "pollutant" under the Clean Air Act, which President Obama is supporting. How much do you think that's going to cost American industry in red tape, taxes, fines, and carbon trading schemes? Consider the latest article of faith among U.S. politicians that what America needs most right now is a new Manhattan Project in search of green energy. Oh really? In the midst of the greatest depression since the 1930s you think it's a good idea to hive off your top scientists, spend billions of tax dollars, and devote huge chunks of your industrial output on a quixotic quest for greener fuel while China is building a new coal-fired power station every five days?

To give you an idea of the crazed, cognitive dissonance that lies ahead of you, allow me a quick weep over what is happening in my country. Our elderly nuclear power stations are on the verge of retirement—but no government, left or right, has dared propose building new ones (well, not until it's far too late: the process takes ten years) for fear of upsetting the Greens.

Our coal stations are besieged by eco-protestors demanding that they be closed. (Al Gore's friend Dr. James Hansen of NASA recently flew over to testify on the protestors' behalf in a court case, arguing that the damage they caused was lawfully excusable because one new power station alone would be responsible for the extinction of 400 species. Amazingly, the judge was persuaded. Expect similar scenes, all too soon, in a court house near you).

Our gas-fired facilities—now that most of our own North Sea supplies have been squandered—are in thrall to crazily fluctuating prices because we don't have sufficient long term storage capacity to weather the market. Worse, it means we are at the mercy of Europe's biggest gas supplier, Russia, which frequently uses gas control as form of economic blackmail.

By 2015—when those nuclear power stations are decommissioned—Britain is going to be in chaos. It will have lost 40 percent of its electricity generating capacity, leading to widespread power failures and black outs. Heating costs will have risen exponentially, causing more deaths among the elderly who need warmth most but can least afford it. The world's fourth largest economy will be in ruins, will have a power supply more akin to Zimbabwe's, and with no energy security because of its dangerous reliance on supplies from dubious countries such as Russia and, almost worse, France. (France is is one of the few countries with the technical know-how to build nuclear plants. They were the ones who built the Osirak nuclear reactor for that nice Saddam Hussein, remember?)

And amid all this impending doom what are our government's plans to save us? Why to build more wind farms (which are expensive, don't work, and blight what little there is left of our beautiful countryside that hasn't been built on to house our soaring population of illegal immigrants); and to commit Britain to an 80 percent reduction in our CO_2 emissions by 2050, which would cripple our economy, close down much of what remains of our industry, and render most motorized transport impossible. This isn't just fiddling while Rome burns; it's rearranging the deck chairs on the *Titanic*, giving up smoking five minutes before you face the firing squad, Hitler in his bunker with the Russians at the gates of Berlin plotting the mighty, great counterattack with non-existent divisions which will squash that damn Stalin once and for all. It's crazier than a fruit bat and madder than a hatter.

"Tough!" you might say. "What do you expect when you allow the Reds and the Greens (and frankly what's the difference?) to take over your country? Like Mark Steyn says, Europe is SO over. It's America alone, now." Problem is, as I mentioned at the beginning, the same crazies who've taken over our government have now taken over yours. We're in this one together, for better or worse. (Worse mostly, I fear. No, I don't fear. I KNOW).

One of the things that has always puzzled me about Greens, as no doubt it has puzzled you, is how people who are supposedly dedicated to all the nice things in life—nature, animals, trees—can yet be so astonishingly vicious, nasty, bullying, and downright fascistic in their policies. It's what makes them such a dangerous political movement. At least with the Nazis you knew where you stood: they were never in it for the peace, love, and harmony. Nor were the Stalinists; nor were the Maoists; nor are the Islamofascists. It's much easier to take a stand against a cause whose values are quite clearly inimical to your own. Much harder when they're whispering gently in your ear idyllic visions of a brighter, cleaner, more natural future where the lion shall lie down with the lamb and those Truffula trees will blossom once more.

Time we returned to those polar bears. It's been a while and you wouldn't want to turn your back on a critter as dangerous as that for too long. Besides, those bears are much more than just bears. They're a symbol, an emblem, a figurehead. Perhaps the single most important thing in the whole eco debate. Capture the polar bear and you've captured the Roman aquila, the Napoleonic eagle: you've destroyed the enemy and won the battle.

Why do you think they were selling all those t-shirts saying *Polar Bears for Obama*? Why was one baby polar bear quoted on a U.S. website as saying: "My Daddy says Sarah Palin doesn't like us"? (Do we believe this by the way? Do we think a baby polar bear really said those exact words? Was it recorded? Were there witnesses?) Why did Leonardo DiCaprio pose with another baby one on the front of *Vanity Fair* for its green issue? Why did Al Gore shoehorn polar bears into *An Inconvenient Truth*? Why has the green lobby campaigned so hard to get the polar bear listed by the U.S. government as an endangered species?

Well, one reason is that a polar bear is not a snail-darter. You remember the snail darter, don't you? The snail darter was that crappy little black and white mottled excuse for a fish—sorry, glorious manifestation of the richness and diversity of God's creation; no less valid in its obscure piscine way than the mighty elephant or the glowing bird of paradise—which managed to hold up the building of a dam on the Tennessee River, after conservationists filed a suit claiming this would exterminate the species.

This was 1973—early days for the eco-bullies and they still had a few lessons to learn. One of them is, if you're going to cry wolf, don't get found out. The dam went ahead and the snail darter did not perish. In fact it has since been reclassified from "endangered species" to "threatened species." A lot of time-and-money-wasting green fuss about nothing then.

The second, more important lesson the Greens had to learn from this episode was, choose your animal species wisely. If you're going to go to the wall, do it for something Joe Public can be made to give a damn about. This rules out most fish (too glassy-eyed, too slimey); all insects and most reptiles (too alien); all snakes and spiders (too scary). Which leaves you with birds (pretty but maybe a bit twittery and fluttery and not that intelligent) and mammals (best option, if you can get one, because they're closest to us).

This is why, you might have noticed, the World Wildlife Fund cannily chose as its emblem the gentle, bamboo chewing, furry, and undeniably lovely panda. And not, say, some particularly rare species of purple and bile-green sea slug.

Was there ever an animal that fit this bill more perfectly than the polar bear? It's white, the color of goodness. (Sorry Mr. President: absolutely no insult intended here. It's a tradition that predates racism.) It's fluffy, it hangs out amid striking scenery, it has the most adorable babies of almost any species imaginable. (Apart from maybe guinea pigs. You ever seen a baby guinea pig? Cuter than the young of a guinea pig has any right to be.) It is what Pat Michaels of the Cato Institute calls a "marquee species"—the kind of creature every right-thinking eco-warrior has dreams about co-opting as his international poster boy.

Just one small problem. The polar bear isn't actually that endangered. In 1950 the global polar bear count stood at around 5,000. Today it is between 20,000 and 25,000. There are those who might reasonably argue that a species which has increased between fourfold and fivefold in a period of six decades is not in catastrophic decline.

Latest surveys tell us that the polar bear picture is, if not universally rosy, certainly nothing to slit our wrists over. A 2006 report by the World Conservation Union found that of nineteen polar bear populations, five were declining, five were stable, two were increasing, and that there wasn't enough data to assess the status of the remaining seven populations. Let us agree then, that there are more immediate and pressing problems for the world than the immediate survival prospects of *Ursus Maritimus*.

This isn't how the eco-campaigners see it, unfortunately. And nor does their amen corner in the international media. When was the last time you opened your newspaper and *didn't* see a picture of a lonely polar bear stranded on a melting ice floe drifting slowly seawards where eventually said bear is supposedly destined to drown? No, I can't remember it either.

Never mind that all the stories about polar bears drowning due to global warming have since been demonstrated to be an urban myth. Yes, some were found drowned once, but it was the result of a freak storm rather than the result of your ongoing, pigheaded refusal to buy yourself an electric car. Hey, though. Why let facts get in the way of a good story.

As Magritte might have said had he been alive today and working for Greenpeace (which as a committed surrealist, he probably would): *Ceci n'est pas un ours polaire.* And he'd be right because polar bears aren't polar bears any more. They've become the official international symbol for ecological correctness. No, worse than that, they've become a substitute for all thought or reason.

Worried your country's economy is going to be screwed by green legislation?

LOOK AT THE PICTURE OF THE POLAR BEAR. SEE HOW WHITE IT IS! HOW FLUFFY!

Concerned that maybe you're not being given all the facts about global warming?

LOOK AT THE LOVELY POLAR BEAR!

Feeling bullied by the Greens?

LOOK AT THE LOVELY POLAR BEAR!

Hey but what about our coal-mining industry?

LOOK AT THE LOVELY POLAR BEAR!

We've been here before and we'll go there again and again. What we are witnessing is yet another classic example of the way the Left, this time in its hand-wringing eco manifestation, substitutes sentiment for intellect, ideology for empiricism, fantasy for reality.

It has decided our planet is in danger from anthropogenic global warming. Therefore the planet IS in danger of anthropogenic global warming, and any evidence to the contrary is counterproductive and must be suppressed.

In November 2008, the Watts Up With That website reported that nearly 180 places in the United States, from Alaska to Alabama, had just recorded their coldest temperatures or heaviest snowfalls on record, based on figures from the National Climate Data Center. As British journalist Christopher Booker has said, declining global temperatures continue to make a mockery of those computer model projections on which the whole global warming scare is based.

Has this made the blindest bit of difference to the views of warmists like James Hansen and Al Gore, or to the policies of their friends in government? Hell no! If anything it has made them more determined to crush dissent.

I didn't dare say this to my BBC wildlife documentary friends on that wonderful trip to the Arctic Circle. But I'm starting to think maybe those polar bears are becoming too dangerous for their own good. It's harsh I know, because I recognize they have many good points. Even so, for the sake of humanity, for the sake of our economies, for the sake of our livelihoods, for the sake of sanity, I believe the time has come to act before it's too late. Let's destroy all the polar bears before they destroy us!

Chapter Seven

CORRUPTING THE YOUNG

A MOVIE WHOSE PREMISE I've never understood is *Indecent Proposal*. This is the one, you'll recall, where rich, handsome Robert Redford offers poor, needy Woody Harrelson a million dollars if only he can spend a night with Harrelson's equally poor, needy wife Demi Moore.

"What?" I want to go every time I watch it. (Actually I've only watched it once. Once was enough. But I hope you'll forgive the rhetorical trope, designed to emphasize how so totally I do not get the movie's premise.) "WHAT?" I go. "And the agonizing moral dilemma inherent in this scenario would be WHAT exactly?"

I mean I'm sorry—call me undiscriminating, call me a whore— but right now I find it pretty hard to think of anyone I wouldn't sleep with for a million dollars. I'm pretty sure my wife (this isn't a reader offer, by the way, this is just a non-legally-binding conjecture) would be exactly the same. We'd do it, either of us, with Kim Jong-il, with Jabba the Hutt, with Michael Moore, if we had to. We'd even make it a foursome with the Elephant Man and the late Andrea Dworkin. Just show us the money (and promise to be gentle) and our services are yours.

Before you put us through this ordeal, though—if it is an ordeal: I never said that we'd be ruling out offers from Liv Tyler—there's something I want to make absolutely clear. We're not doing this because we're money-grubbing harlots. We're doing this for our son. A million dollars is roughly what it will cost us to put our Boy through private school. A million dollars is what we shall have to spend, even at the cost of ruining our lives.

In fact it has come pretty close to ruining our lives already. I'm not asking you to reach for your hankies here—we're free (-ish) citizens; it was our decision—but I do want to let you know some of the sacrifices we're prepared to make for our son's education because I want you to know WHY we make them. We don't take holidays abroad any more; we don't have a pension plan; my wife doesn't get to shop for clothes and accessories like she used to (female readers will understand just how grave an indication of crisis this is); we never go out for dinner (and get really embarrassed when friends suggest meeting at a restaurant because it can only work if they pay); we've got no spare money for emergencies; I worry so much I get insomnia—really bad patches of it, one of which lasted for eighteen months. Just how dumb are we?

Not dumb at all I'd say, and I know a lot of parents reading this are going to feel exactly the same way. There's no privation so great that you're not prepared to suffer on your children's account; where they're concerned, only the best will do.

Here are some are the reasons I like Boy's private school: they've a really nice choir and they sing proper old hymns with rousing traditional tunes in their chapel; there's a thriving reptile club (fifty boys own snakes—corn snakes mainly, though there's also a school Rainbow Boa which bit me on the chin when I was being shown round the school by the headmaster. I said: "You've got to give my boy a place now or I'll sue."); the boys are all instilled with impeccable manners, opening doors for ladies, looking you in the eye when they firmly shake your hand; it has a polo club, which we don't use because the additional costs are too expensive and because Boy is allergic to horses, but which is a wonderfully effective irritant when you're talking about the school to left-wing friends; apart from us, all the other parents seem to be Russian oligarchs, African princes, Eastern industrial magnates, Masters of the Universe bankers, World Champion Golfers, and so on, which presumably means Boy will make lots of spiffy social connections which will serve him well in the future.

But you know what? If you took all these things away, the swimming pool, the climbing wall, the rugger pitches, the Lamborghinis in the parking lot, I'd still think it was money well spent. It's not the facilities, I'm buying into, and it's certainly not the snob thing (the kids and parents at my daughter's state school are just as nice). What counts is the ethos, for—with some notable exceptions—private schools are the only institutions left in Britain which still understand what a liberal education truly means.

By liberal, I don't of course mean in the modern sense of "tofu-munching, tradition-hating, down-dumbing panty-waist" but the exact opposite. I mean NOT progressive. "Progressive" ideas are the very worst thing that ever happened to education. They're the reason one in five British eleven-year olds is innumerate and illiterate, the reason why L.A. schools police are now authorized to carry shotguns, the reason I'm not going skiing (again) this year and the reason school kids in the United States, in Britain, and in most of Europe and Australasia are doomed to be overtaken in every international academic (and later economic) league table by kids from countries that don't believe in progressive education (countries like India and China).

Let's put a few of those "progressive" ideas under the micro-scope and squirm at what we see. Hmm. I have a particularly unpleasant specimen from my country called "non-competitive sports days." This was a tradition invented some time in the Seventies or Eighties by left-wing teachers concerned that any child who came second, third, fourth, or fifth in the egg-and-spoon race would have his (or her) self-esteem irreparably damaged, and that consequently it would be better to ban competitive sports in school altogether.

In the mid-2000s, a UK government-funded body called Sport England (although in this case, perhaps Non Sport England would have been more appropriate) produced a leaflet suggesting suitable activities. "The trouble with traditional sports days is that too many youngsters are left out as spectators," it said. (Yeah. Good point. Let's ban the Super Bowl, ban the World Series, ban the FA Cup Final: it's SO unfair on all the guys watching that they can't be on the pitch playing.) Among the twenty-eight games it proposed was one called "bean bag pick up" and "stranded-sheep"—all carefully designed so that "pupils of lower ability are not exposed."

Now hang on just a second. Let's read that last sentence again. A UK government-funded body is urging schools to play games in which pupils of lower ability are not exposed. Where's the fun in that? Where's the point in that? Surely the whole idea about games—the reason they're exciting, the reason we make an effort, the reason they matter so very much—is precisely this key point that if we don't win, we lose. And losing sucks.

Don't know about you but, me, I WANT my kids to know that losing sucks. Big time. If my kids aren't made to understand, from an early age, that losing sucks they might acquire a taste for it. They'll end up with no ambition and shitty, no-hope jobs and no money and no future. Then I'll have to bail them out with the money I'd hoped to spend on my retirement. And they'll spend it all on heroin probably. Then I'll have to pay for the drying-out clinic. And I'll probably have to bring up their kids, which will be nice in its way, but damned exhausting for a couple in their seventies. No really, if the price to be paid to avert all that future misery, expense, and pain is for my kids, early on in their life, to find themselves riddled with the self-disgust and abject despair which comes from not winning the three-legged race, well that's a sacrifice I'm prepared to make.

And these aren't the pronouncements of some mighty *Victor Ludorum* (that's "winner of the games" for those of you who didn't get Latin in school) you're reading here. At school, I was what we used to call a total spaz. When two captains were taking turns to choose who was going to be in their team, I was always the booby who got picked last. In games of cricket, I was the one in the outfield making daisy chains or day-dreaming about how cool it would be if the Russians invaded and I had a secret Harrier Jump Jet that I knew how to fly and I could lead the Resistance despite just being the pasty-faced schoolboy who everyone thought was crap. In games of football (what you'd call soccer) I was the one that didn't tackle because tackling hurts. Ditto rugger. I came last in all the running races. I could barely swim a length. Just the kind of kid, all those lefties would say, whose "lower ability" ought not to be exposed—to preserve my self-esteem.

But my "lower ability" at sport WAS exposed. All the ruddy time. And did it damage me? You bet it did. It gave me a scar deeper, more painful, more permanent even than the one on Harry Potter's forehead. What that scar told me was: "Forget about being a footballer on $100,000 a week. Forget about all the babes you might attract as an international tennis star or an Olympics gold-medal-winning athlete. You are a spaz. You have no natural sporting talent whatsoever. Accept your inner geek."

So I did accept my inner geek and look where it has got me. Yeah, okay, point taken. But it's certainly got me a lot further than

I would have done if some well-meaning teacher had urged me to "follow my dream" and I'd tried becoming a golf pro instead. Being a complete spaz is not a cruel indication of the world's manifest injustice. It's God's way of telling you you're not cut out to be the next Mark Spitz or Muhammad Ali.

In my book that's a good thing. A healthy thing. A charitable thing. And just because I personally never got an ounce of satisfaction out of competitive school sports doesn't mean I'd ever wish them banned. Where would that leave the thick kids, the morons—and face it, your typical world class sportsman isn't usually the sharpest tool in the box—who are good at absolutely nothing EXCEPT sports? Never mind my self-esteem as a spaz. What about theirs? How are they going to feel if the one annual occasion in their life when they truly get to shine is snatched away from them by some well-meaning lefty?

A measure introduced to make things fairer turns out to make things less fair. Hmm. Now where have we heard that one before? It's one of the things I find almost charming about the liberal-left ideology—the way it's not just mistaken in a few of its notions here and there, but consistently, overwhelmingly, comprehensively wrong about absolutely everything. A World Wide Weltanschauung of Wrong.

At least it would be charming—in its comically barmy way—if it weren't so insidious. When leftists wish to destroy a conservative's arguments they invariably circumvent the troublesome process of actually engaging with them by caricaturing them as "right-wing rant." If right-wingers do more than their share of ranting though, there's probably one very good reason for it. It's because they're in a perpetual state of hair-tearing despair that a counter-ideology of such manifest illogicality and counter-productivity can yet have been able to exert so powerful a grip on society.

Nowhere is this more evident than in the field of education, where, thanks in Britain to the indoctrination of teacher training colleges, and in America to the dubious legacy of progressives like

John Dewey, the ideology of the liberal left goes all but unchallenged.

(Incidentally, Dewey's 1916 book *Democracy and Education* was voted by a panel of conservative thinkers polled by *Human Events* magazine the fifth most harmful book of the twentieth century, after *The Communist Manifesto, Mein Kampf, Quotations from Chairman Mao,* and *The Kinsey Report.*)

Central to this is the rejection of the literary canon (too Dead-White-Male-centric), of rote learning (too Gradgrindian), of rigor (too elitist), of discipline (too hierarchical), nay of the very act of teaching itself. Children, runs the strain of thought—popularized by Dewey, but pioneered as early as the 1840s by another American "reformer" Horace Mann—are such delicate flowers that to try to teach them is to destroy all their creativity and spontaneity. A teacher's true role, then, is not to teach a child but to enable that child to discover knowledge for itself, almost by osmosis.

In fact in today's topsy-turvy educational world, even the acquisition of knowledge is considered unnecessary and passé. What counts nowadays is not that our kids should know stuff; merely that they should understand how to "access" it on the Internet, and then be able to interpret this information according to the politically correct precepts of our day, namely: environmentalism, peace and gender studies, and, above all, cultural relativism.

It's to spare Boy at least some of this modish nonsense that I'm sending him to private school. I suppose "modish nonsense" is just the kind of phrase a conservative *would* splutter about any way of thinking that seems trendy, new-fangled, or anti-traditional. But there's a reason why we conservatives are so attached to tradition. It's because tradition is what has survived over time and been proven to work; bad ideas generally fail, though they recur whenever left-liberals rediscover them.

I'm very much the beneficiary of old school traditions. I was lucky enough to have been sent to a traditional English prep school run by traditional English teachers—many of whom had fought in the war—who believed in teaching traditional subjects the traditional way. We learned history, for example, as an exciting narrative peopled mainly by figures of high rank—Kings and Queens, Princes and Popes, Warriors and other Heroes—and characterized by battles and struggles for power, and punctuated throughout by important, never-to-be-forgotten dates.

A lot of it, thrillingly, seemed to consist of violent and unnatural death. We learned that the fifteenth century Duke of Clarence drowned in a butt of Malmsey wine; that King Henry I perished after eating "a surfeit of lampreys" (that's a kind of blood-sucking fish); that when Mary Queen of Scots was executed the axe man botched the job by taking at least two blows to kill her (then further shocked onlookers when, as he held up the severed head it separated from its hair and tumbled from his grasp, for the once famously beautiful Queen had been wearing a wig); that, best of all, King Edward II was murdered by having a red-hot poker thrust up his backside. ("And how did he die?" one of us asked, all wide-eyed innocence, on a prep-school visit to the site of his murder, Berkeley Castle. But the guide was wise to this one. "He was burnt internally," he replied.)

This is not how history is taught any more. Not, at least in my country's state schools system, and not in yours either. Now history might more appropriately be called "Guilt and Oppression Studies." No longer is it a means of instilling in our children pride at our nations' many great achievements, nor of teaching them about heroic personal examples which they can emulate. Rather it is about discrediting the dead white male patriarchy (George Washington: dope grower; slave owner), bigging up the neglected little guys (non-royal women, non-whites, peasants, etc.) and generally encouraging a sense of shame at having had the temerity and selfishness to have been born in a country with slightly more of a global influence than Switzerland.

It's the same strain of liberal self-hatred noted by Elie Kedourie in an essay on anti-Western bias in the work of that dismal English historian Arnold Toynbee. Kedourie calls it: "The shrill and clamant voice of English radicalism, thrilling with self-accusatory and joyful lamentation. *Nostra culpa, nostra maxima culpa:* we have invaded, we have conquered, we have dominated, we have exploited." It is, as Roger Kimball recently reminded us, another classic case of what James Piereson called "Punitive liberalism."

But there's more to it than mere auto-flagellation. The second, no less dangerous element is its obsession with "value relativism." Which is to say, there is no such thing any more as an authoritative, trustworthy position on the past. Rather, all views are equal since history is just a matter of opinion and everyone should be allowed their say.

In an essay for a pamphlet called *The Corruption of the Curriculum* (Civitas), an English history teacher of thirty-two years experience, Chris McGovern, gave an example from the Labour-approved Schools History Project, whose syllabus is now followed by more than a third of English history pupils. A work pack entitled "World Terrorism since 9/11" contained thirteen sources.

He wrote: "Four of these are about Osama Bin Laden, including one source that provides extracts from his own words across a range of topics and another source that transcribes his words about the September 11th attack. These two pro-Bin-Laden sources are 'balanced' only by a fairly neutral biography of Bin Laden and by a copy of the FBI Wanted poster for him. Across the other nine sources two are pro-US, two are anti-US and four are, broadly, neutral. The final source provides 16 quotations from the world press on the third anniversary of 9/11. Eight of these press reports come from the Islamic world and are largely hostile to the West. The other eight are from Europe and Asia. Five of them are critical of the US. The US press is not represented."

There are many strong reasons to objecting to this approach, not the least of which is that it's incredibly boring. Fifteen- and sixteen-year old kids do not want to know that history is but a complex series of ever changing and equally valid viewpoints. That stuff can come later, if they bother to study it at university. By then, if they're properly educated beforehand, they can reject such piffle for what it is. Till then, they need history as it used to be taught—as a sweeping narrative filled with color, dramatic events, and larger-than-life characters (many, if not most of them, white and of European origin). They should learn classical history, they should learn European history, and they should learn a plain truth about British and American history: that we have done an awful lot of good in the world, including and especially during our military conquests. History taught this way, with dates and time-lines to be memorized, is more comprehensible and more accurate than the politically correct drivel and "values relativism" they're getting now. It's also more fun.

In my head, stuck forever, no matter how many brain cells I've contrived to murder over the year with alcohol, are certain key dates. I know that the Battle of Hastings was in 1066; that Crecy was in 1346 and Agincourt in 1415; that Trafalgar was in 1805 and Waterloo in 1815. Why? Because my history teacher at prep school made me learn it, and at that age—see also times tables—the stuff you learn you'll always retain.

And I'm eternally grateful all that factual knowledge is there because it enables me to do a lot of things I otherwise couldn't do. I can perform quite well in quizzes (once I won a pair of Eurostar tickets to Paris; another time I won a $200 bottle of vintage Krug champagne); I can use information I do know to infer facts that I don't. Like, say, though I don't know Henry V's exact dates, I'm never going to be too far out because I know he won the battle of Agincourt; I have chronological building blocks on which to base, if I wish, an ever-more-detailed understanding of the whole of the

first Millennium AD. I can put current events in an historical perspective. I can value what is great and admirable in my country and
know when some socialist schemers are trying to deny me what
should by rights be mine: the ancient liberties of England (or the
freedoms America defended at Yorktown and at the Alamo, and
on the battlefields of Europe and the Pacific). Boy, I hope, receiv-
ing a similar education to the one I had, will be able to do this too.
Such a gift is damned near worth a half million dollars already.

But this is much bigger than Boy, of course. Much, much,
MUCH bigger. If I say it's about the whole future of Western Civilization it's not because I'm expecting him to become Prime Minister or President—(mind you, for that kind of money, maybe I
should)—but because I believe it is incumbent upon us conservatives, a moral duty, to do everything in our power to fight against
this erosion of our values and stand up for what we believe.

I'm thinking here especially of the problem Allan Bloom
addressed in *The Closing of the American Mind*. It opened:
"There is one thing a professor can be absolutely sure of: almost
every student entering the university believes, or says he believes,
that truth is relative. If this belief is put to the test one can count
on the student's reaction: they will be uncomprehending."

The virus has spread to Britain. In her characteristically elo-
quent and hard-hitting polemic *All Must Have Prizes*, Melanie
Phillips quotes an Oxford university don, Marianne Talbot, on the
effects of relativism on her undergraduates. "Many of the young
have been taught to think *their* opinion is no better than anyone
else's, that there is no *truth*, only truth-for-me. . . . The young have
been taught, or so it seems, that they should never think of the
views of others as false, but only as *different*. They have been
taught that to suggest someone else is wrong is at best rude and
at worst immoral."

What's wrong with these non-judgemental attitudes? Well, for
one thing, they're non-judgemental. Many years ago, in the days

before kids were encouraged to check in their brains at the college gatehouse, judgement used to be considered one of the noblest and most demanding skills a man could acquire. Judgement was the wisdom Solomon showed when he threatened to cut that baby in half, knowing that the child's blood mother would never allow this to happen. Good judgement was the ability to make sound decisions based on a lifetime's accumulated experience. Bad judgement was for fools. No judgement was for the spineless, the childish, and the mentally deficient. If you'd called someone judgemental any time before 1960, they would have shaken their head in puzzlement, then assumed it was a compliment.

Not any more. Conservatives often like to imagine that to win the war, all you need to do is win the big battles over key issues like national security and the economy. Liberals know better than that. What really counts, they realize, are not the cities but the secret supply trails leading through the jungle to Dien Bien Phu: the minds of the young, the way they are taught, no, better than that—the very language itself. He who controls the dictionary holds the key to the citadel. No coincidence, I think, that Chomsky's specialty is linguistics.

Note, for example, the way the Left has managed to capture one of the most cherished words in the conservative lexicon—freedom—and subvert it to its own ends. Freedom used to mean the same thing as liberty. Now it is often used in the antithetical, Collectivist sense, of "entitlement to services administered by the state"; "freedom from discrimination"; "freedom from poverty"; "freedom from injustice."

George Orwell, alleged socialist though he may have been, was on to this trick as early as 1949 when he wrote his appendix to *1984*. One of the most effective ways of suppressing heretical thought, he explained, was to eliminate undesirable words or strip them of their meaning. The example he gave was "free." The word continued to exist in Newspeak (the official language of Big

Brother, his imaginary totalitarian state) but only in the sense of "This field is free from weeds" or "The dog is free from lice"— never in the sense of "politically free" or "intellectually free."

Another English author, E. M. Forster, once famously wrote: "Only connect!" (I'm really sorry about all this name-dropping, by the way. But did I ever say an education stopped you being an annoying smartarse?) And it all does connect. The twisting of the lexicon; the growth of cultural relativism; the denigration of tradition; the rejection of authority; the abandonment of knowledge— these are not just the random by-products of having smoked too much dope in the Sixties, or having attended too many anti-globalization demos, or having spent too much time with brown corduroy jackets with leather patches on the arm. They're part of a consistent, well-thought-out, comprehensive, and devastatingly effective program to destroy Western Civilization from within.

If you doubt this, take a look at the career of Bill Ayers, Barack Obama's friend, a founder of the radical Weatherman Underground, which set off bombs at the Pentagon, the U.S. Capitol, and police headquarters in New York City in the early 1970s. He is now of course a professor of Education at the University of Illinois and is a prominent "reformer" of your public school system, especially if you happen to live in Chicago. His kind is legion, the radicals of the Sixties and Seventies are now tenured professors teaching your kids and mine.

You and I might have thought, as rational conservatives, that Sixties radicalism had played itself out. But it hasn't. From its redoubts in higher education, its menace has only taken on respectability, spread, and become an orthodoxy. We made a big mistake in just loathing the Left and not getting inside the mind of our enemy; we should have been like World War II generals— Rommel and Montgomery before El Alamein, maybe—with one another's photographs on the walls of our campaign tents, the better to understand our foe.

All that crazy drivel those French structuralist, post-structuralist, and post-post-structuralist philosophers started writing from the Fifties onwards; all that trendy stuff Chomsky wrote about linguistics. I'm not saying you should actually read any of it—

Jesus, what kind of sadist do you think I am? But what I am saying is that just because something smells like bullshit and in fact IS bullshit doesn't mean that it can't also be employed as a deadly biological weapon to kill you, your family, and everything you hold dear.

The fact that Derrida, Foucault, Chomsky—indeed 90 percent of academics generally—are opaque to the point of incomprehensibility is a weapon not a weakness. It's designed to make people like us take our eye off the ball: to make us go "Yikes! This is so boring I don't want to know." It means their arguments can never be contradicted (because no one, not even the authors possibly, ever knew what they meant in the first place). It creates a new kind of language which makes politically sympathetic initiates feel part of the club, while keeping those unsympathetic to the cause well away. (Only the committed are ever going to try wading through that kind of pseudo-intellectual gibberish.) Above all, it pulls the rug from under the feet of all the scholars and academics who have gone before, and subverts higher education for a specific political end.

It never used to be this way. For generations—since time immemoriam, indeed—scholars have always seen their purpose as being a disinterested quest for knowledge. Building on the work of earlier scholars, and on their own studies, experiments, and observations, their aim was to expand the sum total of human knowledge—and to share that knowledge with their fellow men, so that they could benefit from it and expand on it. For this reason, they sought to express themselves as clearly as they could. With good reason did Aristotle convey his thoughts in a literary style praised by Cicero as "a river of gold": being a sensible chap,

Aristotle had worked out that posterity stood a better chance of appreciating his wisdom if it were conveyed lucidly, attractively, and comprehensibly than if that wisdom were conveyed in a new, made-up jargon language comprising squeaks, grunts, and humming noises.

The new academia dispenses with all that altruistic nonsense. And with all that clarity nonsense too. If a modern academic can be understood then he has to all intents and purposes failed, for it means he is still shackled by the values of the discredited past.

Foremost among these discredited values—in the eyes of modern academe—is the concept that so appalled all Allan Bloom's right-thinking students and continues to appal their right-thinking successors today: absolutism. No longer is it permissible in academe to argue with any forcefulness that some ideas are better than other ideas; that some cultures have more to teach us than other cultures; that some books are greater than other books; that there are certain universal moral values which ought to be disseminated as widely as possible, and other value systems that are wrong and ought to be exposed as such.

This is exactly the kind of lame, specious, maddeningly-wrong-in-so-many-different ways faux-thought that I don't ever want to hear Boy brandishing at me over breakfast one morning. (And yet another reason why that million dollars—if I can raise it—will be so well spent). It's not that I won't be able to demolish his arguments in moments—C'mon: it's hardly a Yale summa-cum-laude challenge is it?—more that I don't want any of his brain-space wasted on such idiocy in the first place.

Sure I'd know he was doing it from the best of motives. (Aaagh! That phrase again! Shall we never escape it?) He'd only be doing out of kindness, fellow feeling, to show that he understood that I have my point of view and he has his point of view and we're all cool, man, because there is no right and no wrong, only differences of opinion, or worse, different truths that each one of us can make for himself. But what, of course, I'd have to explain to him with a weary paternal sigh is this: "Smooth, easy, inoffensive down to Hell."

"Eh, Dad?"

"Milton. John Milton. Poet you've never heard of. Comes from a poem he wrote called *Paradise Lost*. But he was being literal, I was being metaphorical."

"Meta-what?"

"Never mind. I'm just talking about the way ideas that are so simple to acquire and so comfortable to hold because they feel so nice can sometimes achieve the opposite ends from the ones they intended."

"You mean, like, they promise you Heaven and they give you Hell?"

"Boy, you may yet be your father's son!"

So then, I suppose, we'd have to go into further detail. Not difficult stuff. Obvious stuff that you and I take for granted but which so many of today's kids don't.

Stuff like: Shakespeare is better than Maya Angelou. And more worthy of study. In fact there's just no comparison. If you had a hundred hours to spend on both, you should put Maya to one side (lovely and warm and meaningful though she surely is), and Sylvia Plath and Derek Walcott and whichever other socially relevant/unjustly neglected/suitably victimish authors you'd been given in order to undercut any of that Dead-White-Male-centrism, and just stick to Shakespeare. He's great. The greatest.

And: Modern Judaeo-Christian civilization is the apogee of human accomplishment. It has cherry picked all that was best about previous great civilizations—most notably, indeed almost exclusively, that of the Greeks and the Romans: the Persians and the Pharaohs and the Ancient Chinese you can frankly keep—and created a society about as just and fair and universally beneficial as any society made up of flawed human beings is ever likely to be. WE ARE THE BEST. Other cultures, well, I wouldn't go so far as to say that they suck; they've definitely got one or two things going for them: the Middle Eastern/Pashtun tradition of hospitality is nice, so's the way the whole African village looks after the kids—but there's a reason why about 99 percent of the world's people would much rather be in our country and not their own. It's because basically we rule. And we shouldn't be ashamed to say so.

"But Dad, that is, like, SO culturally imperialistic of you. So elitist. Racist probably too."

"Enough of your stupid–ists, already. And why are you speaking like an American? You're supposed to be English."

"Yeah well you're sounding pretty American too, I have to say."

"You're right. It's something I do quite a lot, I've noticed. All those 'sos' and 'likes' and 'like totallys' and 'this rules' and 'that sucks,' it's like I kind of feel so awkward talking about intellectual ideas that I try to make them more accessible by pretending I'm in an episode of *Friends. Beavis and Butthead*, even. But you know what? I think this is another facet of what Allan Bloom was talking about. Our culture is now so comprehensively dumbed down that even the educated are fearful of sounding too clever. Damn those liberal-lefties! I thought I was immune but they've even got through to me."

"Nice digression, Dad, but it's not going to go down well with your American audience. They're now going to think you equate talking American with being stupid."

"Oh for goodness sake, they're conservative Americans. They're more intelligent than to buy into all that liberal-style offense-taking bull. Anyway it's not what I meant."

"Sorry was this conversation heading anywhere in particular?"

"Yes. Thanks for reminding me. I was about to get to the key point of the whole chapter."

"Which is?"

"That if you really believe that everything has equal value, what you're also saying is that nothing has any value. And if the values of your culture are no better or worse than those of any other culture, that presumably means you believe there is nothing in your society worth defending."

"War's always been more your bag than mine, Dad."

"So you'd agree would you, that a democracy with universal suffrage, freedom of speech, property rights, a welfare safety net, and a functioning market economy is no better or worse than, say, an Islamic theocracy where homosexuals are buried alive, women who've been gang raped get hanged for adultery, girls are denied an education, and thieves have their hands chopped off?"

"I thought this chapter was about education."

"It is about education. It's about how the cultural and moral relativism introduced by generations of liberal leftists are a missile aimed directly at the heart of everything in our world that is most good and noble and right. It will destroy our glorious traditions of free speech and free enquiry, our notions of quality and value. It will smother the productive competitiveness that leads to excellence. It will handicap the talented, and cosset the mediocre. It will make our country poorer, both culturally and economically. It will induce a sense of shame where we ought to feel proud. It will debase the achievements of all the hardworking men and women who have gone before us. It will enable our rivals to overtake us. And if they so wish—as some of them do—to destroy us."

"Heavy shit, Dad."

"Wait. There's more."

"You don't think, maybe this chapter has gone on long enough?"

"It is a worry, certainly. But I hope I've made it varied enough—this dialogue device, for example—and broached sufficient worthwhile ideas to keep my readers hanging in there just a while longer. Besides there's one more really quite important thing I wanted to say about progressive educational theory."

"What's that?"

"It doesn't work."

"Not at all?"

"Not one teeny tiny bit."

"That's very sweeping."

"True, though, for it all stems from one totally self-defeating principle. The mistrust of didactism. The idea that teaching doesn't work."

"But how can you teach someone without, er, teaching them."

"My point exactly, but you'd be amazed by how many in the educational establishment on both sides of the Atlantic have failed to grasp this. It's how the liberal-left works unfortunately. Being idealists, they think up their theories first and then try to apply them in the real world. Whereas we conservatives—that's me, and I hope you one day—are pragmatists who prefer to look at the world as it really is and then develop our systems accordingly."

"Gosh. Can you give me an example of that?"

"Indeed I can, which is why I put that feeder question into your mouth just then. It has to do with that most basic of all educational necessities: the ability to read."

"Like you taught me to do."

"Quite. Your sister too. And do you know, of all things I've achieved in my life—and I've done some pretty cool stuff: not being eaten by great white sharks, publishing five novels, travelling overland from the top to bottom of Africa, throwing a cherry tomato at a moving squirrel on the garden wall at thirty yards range the other day and hitting him bang on the head—nothing I've done or ever will do is going to give me the same satisfaction."

"You're sounding mawkish, Dad."

"Can't help it, Boy. Teach your kid to read and you give him the key to almost everything that matters: self-worth; social competence; education; intellectual freedom; a half-way decent job; empathy; understanding; an ability to get lost for hours on end in another universe; an excuse to chat up the very attractive person in the café you've just spotted reading *War and Peace*, because, hey, like, you think it's a great book too ... "

"Urrgh. You mean, like, a girl?"

"Wait till you're older. Now, can you remember how I taught you to read."

"Yeah. With that book. *Superphonics*. The one with Jen the Hen and Zug the Bug."

"Exactly. Then you'll remember how it worked. It broke up every word into sounds called 'phonemes' and once you'd learned what all the phonemes were, you could read any sentence in the English language."

"If you say so. Don't remember it being that complicated. A bit repetitive maybe."

"It isn't complicated and it is repetitive. That's how it sticks in your brain. It's called 'synthetic phonics' and every experiment there has ever been from 1918 onwards has shown it be by far the most effective way there is to teach children to read. You don't need any special skills to teach it. And it's completely class blind and color blind. There's a school in one of the poorest districts of inner London, where 90 percent of kids are Bangladeshis from homes where little or no English is spoken, yet they all read perfectly with literacy levels that are on average twenty-two months ahead of national norms. They're taught using synthetic phonics."

"Isn't everybody?"

"No."

"Why not?"

"That thing I mentioned earlier. Progressive educationists are more interested in nice-sounding ideas that don't work than they are in boring-sounding ideas that do work. And it is even worse in America than it is over here. In the United States most kids are taught to read using a method called 'Look and Say,' which was invented in eighteenth century France to teach deaf children to read. It all goes back to Rousseau's ideas of natural development, to the reforms of Horace Mann, and to a futile debate about whether the act of reading is or isn't inseparable from comprehension, but you don't need to know the tedious details. The point is that because of bad political ideas British and American kids—especially kids from poorer backgrounds where there isn't a culture of reading—are having their educational future sabotaged right from the word go.'"

"Can I watch TV now?"

"No. I want to give you one other example—to do with Math, this time—which I want to include because I think it will make my American conservative readers' blood boil. You remember that film *Stand and Deliver*?"

"If it wasn't made by Pixar I'm not interested."

"It wasn't. It was movie based on the true story of a Bolivian immigrant named Jaime Escalante, who made a name for himself in the late Seventies by teaching Math to mostly poor Hispanic kids at a rough Los Angeles high school to a level where eighteen of them passed the Advanced Placement calculus exam. When they passed, the Educational Testing Service assumed they must have cheated, because ghetto kids don't do calculus. So they retook the test, under tighter supervision this time, and still they passed."

"How come?"

"Because being Bolivian—from a poor country where trendy theories like child-centered teaching, and special pleading for oppressed minority groups, and discovery-based approaches to learning don't apply—he just got on and taught the kids in the traditional way. When asked what his secret was, Escalante said: 'You have to emphasize the basics.' "

"I thought you said this story was going to make conservative readers' blood boil."

"I haven't got to the annoying bit, yet. Escalante's method works but still hardly any teachers use it in California these days. It's just not as sexy as theories like "ethnomathematics," which was designed to counteract the inherent cultural imperialism of traditional math and replace it with teaching methods more attuned with the pupil's ethnic culture."

"Bet it's really going to take off in countries like India and China. Because they SO need that extra leg-up"

"Yeah, me too, Boy. But you've started saying ironic, knowing things you'd never say in real life because you're only a child."

"I know Dad. That's because you made this conversation up. It's just your fantasy of what might have happened if you hadn't put me through all those expensive private schools. But you did, didn't you?"

"Indeed I did son. It's an amazing story which I might tell you some day. It all started when I wrote a slightly flippant essay in an American book in which I offered my sexual services in return for the million dollars I needed to pay for your education. And you'll never guess what. About a month later, I got this very nice letter from a group of lovely ladies called Meg Ryan, Scarlett Johansson, Liv Tyler, Claire Danes, and one or two others.

"Dear Mister Delingpole," it began. "As huge admirers of your witty style, if not necessarily your politics...."

Chapter Eight

THE GREAT WHITE LIBERAL DEATH WISH

GOD, I HATE BEING A WHITE MAN. Every morning I throw myself out of bed and dash to check in the mirror just in case some wonderful transformation has taken place in the night. But it never has. Still no beautiful, almond eyes. Still no lithe, honey-colored physique. Still no clever, anti-reflective, non-burning skin. Still no enormous, great, big, thwacking monster of a . . . uh . . . brain.

And as I stare disconsolately at my irredeemably WASPish features, I think to myself: if only I could jump; if only I could sprint; if only I had a natural sense of rhythm; if only I weren't so stupid and responsible for all the world's ills. Then what I do is walk on down the hall to my sun tan machine, turn the dial up to 11 and. . . .

No, no. I jest. I don't really feel bad about being a white man—any more, I hope, than I'd feel bad if I were a black, or a brown, or a yellow man. The French have a wonderful phrase to describe someone who feels good about himself, who is well balanced, comfortable, and content with his lot: "*se sentir bien dans sa peau.*" It translates literally as "to feel well in one's skin." If we don't feel well in our skin we're in deep trouble. Look at what happened to dear old Michael Jackson.

All this seems obvious and oughtn't need mentioning, except I've noticed of late that one or two of my fellow whities have been having serious trouble coming to terms with their ethnicity. And I thought, by way of therapy—free therapy, which is damned generous of me, given how much some of these guys earn—I might offer them a few words of encouragement.

There's poor Michael Moore, for example. Correction, very rich Michael Moore. He's got it really bad. He hates himself so much he wrote a book called *Stupid White Men*—eagerly bought by millions of other white people: go figure. He's also stupid enough to think his Twin Towers joke was clever—the one about how the Towers would still be standing if those four planes had been full of blacks instead of whites, because the terrorists would have been crushed by the dudes, who as we all know take no disrespect from nobody. A columnist we have in London called Yasmin Alibhai Brown—usually so PC she makes Maureen Dowd sound like Rush Limbaugh—actually walked out of his show in disgust when he tried that here in London. Bit of a booboo there Mikey, do you not maybe think? Insulting to those black people who died on the 9/11 flights. Insulting to the white people who died on the 9/11 flights. And not wholly supportable in the light of what we know about Flight 93, where all that we-don't-take-no-shit-from-no-one-motherfucker behavior you so applaud, was coordinated by a white guy named Todd Beamer.

But Mikey is by no means alone with his little problem. It is shared in Britain by a man named Greg Dyke who, until quite recently was Director General (head honcho) of the BBC—an institution he described as "hideously white." It is also shared in the United States, I've noticed, by every white liberal columnist who has ever written about the "browning of America" in tones of such salivating glee you're left in no doubt whatsoever that this is just what whitey has coming to him, and a darned good thing too.

Yep, it all looks worryingly similar to that streak of lacerating self-hatred we noticed earlier in the chapter on the Green movement. It's like watching Dobby the House Elf bashing his own head with a book in the Harry Potter films. "*Bad* Dobby. *Bad* Dobby.*" Now I'm no Dobby fan. In fact, I think he may well be the second most annoying character ever to appear in a kids' movie, after Jar Jar Binks. But even I, a Dobby-skeptic, find that relentless masochism too much to bear. "Lighten up, Dobby," I want to go. "Sure you look like a low-budget Gollum. Sure you're incredibly irritating. But stop beating yourself up so much. You're diligent, you're loyal, Hermione thinks you're great."

It's what I'd like to say to all those self-hating white guys too. "Look Mikey, Greg, white liberal columnists everywhere, I can't pretend I don't occasionally wish on you the same fate Dobby suffers at the hands of [reader warning: crucial, Harry-Potter-related plot giveaway approaching] Bellatrix Lestrange in *The Deathly Hallows*. But look on the bright side. It's not like us loathsome, worthless white guys have achieved exactly zilch these last few millennia. For example, we.... "

Then, I'd give them a few examples. The complete works of Shakespeare. The theory of relativity. The Acropolis. The U.S. Constitution. Magna Carta. Habeas Corpus. Any number of other admirable things with Latin names, too numerous to mention. And ones with Greek names, because the Greeks were white-enough too, weren't they? *Citizen Kane*. *The Simpsons*. The vacuum cleaner. *War and Peace*. *Stairway to Heaven*. The discovery of DNA. The Renaissance. The Protestant work ethic. Woody

Allen. Leonardo Da Vinci. The piano. Baseball. Monopoly. The jack rabbit vibrator. Defibrillators. Helicopters. The flushing toilet. The postage stamp. The Internet. The moon landings. The theme tune to *Hawaii Five-O*.

After that, I like to think they'd all feel a teeny tiny bit better. If they didn't I could always go on some more. I could maybe mention:

The Goldberg Variations; *Being John Malkovich*; *South Park*; the telephone; penicillin; TV; the theory of gravity; taxonomy; The Authorized Version of the Bible (the King James Version to you); *The Wealth of Nations*; Goethe; Moliere; Janacek; Sibelius; Tchaikovsky; Rachmaninov; Ibsen; Chekhov; Sir Isaac Newton; Sir Christopher Wren; *The Three Musketeers*; the Three Stooges; Laurel and Hardy; Alcock and Brown (the British pilots who made the first non-stop transatlantic crossing by air); Gilbert and Sullivan; Crosby, Stills, Nash & Young.

And by this stage, I like to think those self-hating white guys might be willing to concede that being white isn't such an awful thing to be and that on balance we've probably contributed more to global civilization than we've stolen from it.

Then again, maybe not. The thing about race, I've noticed, is that it's a subject almost no one is prepared to discuss openly, or honestly.

It's a bit like Larry Summers's getting into such trouble at Harvard for having hinted that women might be genetically less well-suited to math and sciences than men are. Never mind that it tallies perfectly with all the latest research by scientists like Simon Baron-Cohen (that's Borat's uncle) at Cambridge University into autism, extreme-male-brain-syndrome, and what used to be called "Engineer's disease." Never mind that it also concurs with almost everything any of us have ever observed since time began. It just happens to be one of those things you're not allowed to say. Why can't you say it? You JUST CAN'T.

Race is just the same, if not even worse. It's a taboo so hedged about with disingenousness, and wishful thinking, and intellectual dishonesty, it's no wonder I'm starting get a little nervous. You see, I'm going to try to discuss the issue of immigration as honestly as I dare. And I'm wondering: will you think I'm evil? Will you think I should maybe join the Ku Klux Klan? Or will you, as I hope, go: "Way to go, James. That's exactly what I think!"

Not that I'm complaining, mind. These taboos on things like sex and race are an absolute gift for us conservative commentators because we can say amazingly obvious things that everyone knows in their hearts to be true and come across like we're incredibly brave and deep and insightful.

Here's my friend Rod Liddle from *The Spectator* on President Obama.

Is he black? I'm not so sure. He has a white mother and a black father, so I suppose he is of mixed race, or what the South Africans used to call "colored." He was, before and during the campaign, many different colors. As a politician in Chicago, he was not regarded as black at all, partly because of his white mum and partly because he had no background in the civil rights struggle of the 1950s and 1960s; nor was he descended from slave stock. This regrettable lack of blackness seemed to count against him early on in the battle against Hillary Clinton, when many African-American voters, and particularly those in the Deep South states, were inclined to line up behind her. Obama became blacker as the battle against John McCain intensified; suddenly America was not simply voting in a presidential election, choosing between a liberal Democrat and a moderate Republican, but doing much much more than that: fulfilling Martin Luther King's dream, showing itself to be a "mature" democracy, lighting a beacon in a sea of eternal darkness, etc., etc. I ought to mention that this was not how Obama

portrayed the contest himself—he was, to his credit, extraordi-
narily averse to be seen playing the race card. No; this was how
it was presented by the media. But, one way or another, by the
final stages of the campaign Obama had morphed into a fully
fledged African-American, hallelujah.

Great, isn't it? I wish I'd written that. Maybe Rod should have
written this book instead of me, except he's a bit conflicted. For
one thing he says he would have voted for Obama himself. For
another, he's a self-proclaimed Lefty. He's not, though, really, I
wouldn't say. On almost every issue he writes about—Islamism,
the Nanny State, feminism—there's barely a cigarette paper's difference between his views and mine. (Our only major disagree-
ments are on Monarchy; Fox Hunting; and Neo-Conservative
Interventionism.) I mention this because I don't want all my
potential left-liberal fans out there to be put off buying this book.
Just because I'm saying your stupid ideology sucks doesn't mean
you won't agree with every word I write. It may be that like Rod,
you only think you are a liberal-lefty because you think it makes
you sound nicer. Or because, also like Rod, it'll help you pull more
chicks.

Anyway, what I like about Rod's little riff there is that he talks
about race with a cheery openness which has become all but ver-
boten in our PC culture. You can't say that Asian kids tend to do
better at math; you can't say East Africans make particularly good
long distance runners; you can't even say—as I got told off for
doing once—that somebody's surname sounds like they might be
Jewish.

Look I like Jews. Many of my best friends are Jews. I often wish
I were Jewish myself. And one of the things that fascinates me
about the Jewish people I know and love and admire is what
makes them so peculiarly Jewish. Because there's something in
there, definitely. It's not just utterly random coincidence that

around 20 percent of all Nobel Prize laureates are Jewish, when
Jews only represent approximately one percent of the world's population. Nor that they're often so talented and so funny and so
clever—way more than the national average, I'd say. Does this
make me anti-Semitic? Does this sound like an editorial from *Der
Sturmer*? Is it but one small step from here to yellow stars and
death camps?

Personally, I reckon no. Those who argue otherwise are playing a classic left-liberal trick: stifling all debate about an issue they
find uncomfortable by simply closing down the argument. You
can't discuss Jewish identity because of the Holocaust. You can't
discuss people's skin color because of slavery. You can't talk about
immigration because if you do you're a racist.

In Britain there was a period of forty years when you couldn't
discuss immigration at all. And all because of a Tory MP named
Enoch Powell. A great classical scholar and famously intelligent,
driven, articulate man beloved by his parliamentary constituents
in the industrial Midlands, he made just one serious error in his
career, which was to cost him his bright political future and his
reputation. He was found guilty of the dread crime of racism.

The occasion was a speech he made in 1968, known ever after
as the Rivers of Blood speech because of a literary allusion to the
poet Virgil made in its most inflammatory passage.

It went:

As I look ahead, I am filled with foreboding. Like the Roman,
I seem to see "the River Tiber foaming with much blood." That
tragic and intractable phenomenon which we watch with horror on the other side of the Atlantic [the racial turmoil and Civil
Rights struggles of the 1960s] but which there is interwoven
with the history and existence of the States itself, is coming
upon us here by our own volition and our own neglect. Indeed,
it has all but come. In numerical terms, it will be of American

proportions long before the end of the century. Only resolute and urgent action will avert it even now.

Powell was talking, in his convoluted, melodramatic way, about the dangers of the unchecked immigration—mostly from black Commonwealth countries like Jamaica—which he believed would end up swamping Britain and distort its national character. This was a concern that the majority of the British public shared: 74 percent of those polled shortly afterwards said they agreed with his speech. Powell was subsequently voted by the readers of one newspaper the most popular politician in the country. Research even suggested that Powell's speech was responsible for gaining his party the 2.5 million extra votes which won it an unexpected victory in the subsequent general election.

His reward for speaking his mind? To be sacked immediately from the cabinet of his Prime Minister—a bloated Whiggish appeaser named Ted Heath; subsequently to sell Britain's interests still further down the river by dragging it into full, costly member-ship of the European Union—and to be reviled ever after as a racist bigot. Even four decades on, it is a suicidally brave British politi-cian who would dare, however cautiously, to suggest that Powell may have had a point. (When a prospective Tory candidate said as much in 2008, he was swiftly encouraged by his party to resign.)

As we shall see in the next chapter, Powell may indeed have had a point. Not about those Commonwealth blacks—now mostly well integrated and as British as roast beef and Yorkshire pud—but about immigrants from another former colony. But even if Powell was totally wrong in his views and utterly despicable, since when has it been the duty of Western liberal democracy to smother full and frank debate about anything? Is not freedom of speech one of the vital qualities that have made Britain (and of course America) great?

This was John Milton's argument in *Areopagitica*—his English Civil War-era tract against censorship and in favor of free speech. Only by exposing all ideas, good or bad, to the test of open discussion can we ever hope to reveal the truth of God. "There must be many schisms and many dissections made in the quarry and in the timber, ere the house of God can be built," he said.

And you don't need to be remotely religious to see the sense in this. John Stuart Mill put the secular case for the same argument in *On Liberty*. We need to be exposed to the full range of opinions for two key reasons, he said. First, because what is kept from us may be true or contain a kernel of truth. Second, because if we allow our opinions to go unchallenged then the truth, severed from its rational roots, becomes enfeebled.

Why should issues as fundamental to the wellbeing of society as race and immigration be considered such dynamite as to be beyond the pale of reasonable discussion?

Search me. I'm with Milton, miserable old Puritan though he was. I think that the worse an idea is—Holocaust denial, say—the more essential it becomes to expose its inadequacies to cool analysis. To suppress it just suggests its opponents might have something to hide.

But I suppose the Left-liberal (and even wet conservative) argument on race and immigration might go something like this: "Look at the slave trade; look at the history of lynchings; look at segregation; look at the way English pubs in the Sixties would have signs saying "No Dogs, Blacks, Irish." Racism is such a terrible thing—and its evils so seductive to so many—that only through the most drastic and repressive measures by the state can its menace ever be successfully eradicated."

To which I say: "Nuts!" Two wrongs do not make a right. The way to give ethnic minorities a better deal is not to give ethnic majorities a worse one. All you create then is resentment. The very resentment that serves only to intensify the racism that your well-meaning policies are trying to extirpate.

There's no better example of this than Affirmative Action—that wonderfully misguided social-healing concept that makes a loser of EVERYONE. Suppose you're an Hispanic or black student who, thanks to a mix of innate talent and hard work, gets into a law school which promotes affirmative action. Do you really want to be sharing course-space with idiots who got there, not because they're as bright as you, but just because they share your skin color? And how are you going to get over that nagging worry at the back of you mind: "Did I really get my place because I'm good? Or because some bleeding-heart law prof wanted to alleviate his white-boy guilt about my ethnic background?" And how are the deserving white and Asian boys and girls who ought to have got on the course but didn't going to feel about this? And isn't it a little bit, well, racist, to bracket people of color into one lumpen, supplicant category marked "oppressed and needy?"— as though they're all so useless the only way they can ever pull themselves up by their bootstraps is through charity and special pleading?

Our problem with skin color is that we dwell on it not nearly enough—but, at the same time, far, far too much. I'll give you an example of the first from the brave and funny young Iranian comic ("I'm a female Iranian stand-up. They call me the box-ticker.") Shappi Khorsandi. She does a sketch about being friends with the only black person in the room at a typical London party, and about how she'll describe him when someone else at the party asks her to point out which one her friend is. "Uh, he's got curly hair. He's wearing a brown jumper...blue jeans...black shoes..., um, red t-shirt..." "Oh. Do you mean the *black* guy?" "Is he? Oh, yes. Never noticed that before...."

Most of us would walk a million miles rather than confront the issue of someone's race either to their face or within their earshot.

It would be nice to think that decades of integration, that heart-warming video of Paul McCartney and Stevie Wonder duetting "Ebony and Ivory," and Benetton's entire poster ad output have successfully combined to make us all so un-hung-up about ethnicity we don't even notice anyone's skin color any more. But it's not that is it? We feel just too damn awkward. And the reason we feel awkward is because we've been taught to feel awkward. It's where the liberal-left wants us: struck dumb with embarrassment.

You'd think the logical way to heal the racial divide would be to break down the barriers, show everyone how delightfully similar we are, how we can all share the same culture as Britons or Americans. But this has never been the liberal-left's way. The liberal-left seeks to emphasize difference: partly because it thinks this will enable oppressed minorities to feel better about themselves, partly because it deliberately exploits ethnic balkanization and identity politics as a means of gaining more votes, and partly because in its own self-hatred it advances a preference for almost any culture other than its own white Western culture.

Black History Month is one example. It was founded in 1926 with the best of intentions—ah, that all too familiar phrase—by black historian Carter G. Woodson, both of whose parents had been former slaves. Originally called Negro History Week, it was designed to raise awareness of black contributions to American history, in an era where few such examples were either known to the public or studied by historians. (This was before Martin Bernal came along and rescued African-American pride once and for all by demonstrating in his magisterial exercise in wishful thinking, *Black Athena*, that the Ancient Greeks were, in fact, black.)

We have something similar over here in my own country, the celebrations centering round the mighty achievements of a hitherto obscure woman named Mary Seacole. Never mind that she wasn't even that black. (Her father was a white Scottish soldier, making her Creole, like Obama.) Never mind that she wasn't nearly in the same league as her great contemporary—the massively influential but unfortunately white and aristocratic hospital reformer, known as The Lady of the Lamp, Florence Nightingale. What mattered was that she was vaguely brown of hue, definitely female, and that she had enjoyed at least reasonable renown in her time, running a popular hotel cum convalescent home for wounded soldiers near the front line during the Crimean War.

A warm, big-hearted, semi-black woman Mary Seacole undoubtedly was, beloved no doubt by many an ailing squaddie. But more worthy of study than Queen Victoria or Queen Elizabeth I? Or the chariot-riding warrior queen Boadicea? Or any of the numerous heroes who helped make Britain great from King Alfred to the Duke of Wellington to Winston Churchill? Not even Seacole's most fervent admirers would try stretching the point that far.

Yet whose face is it that stares from the minuscule history book section at my daughter's primary school? Mary Seacole's. Whose exploits are celebrated for a full month in a special display at our local lending library? Mary Seacole's. Who takes up probably more space in the average British junior state school curriculum than all the other world's historical figures put together? I think you can guess the answer.

I have nothing personally against Mary Seacole. My beef is with what she has come to represent: a naïve and socially poisonous doctrine that only through a form of state-sanctioned separatism can ethnic minorities gain self-esteem.

Are we really to believe that the outlook of black schoolchildren is so limited, and their power of imagination so feeble, that the only historical figures with whom they can properly identify are those with the same skin tone? Is there not—as with affirmative action—something inherently racist about such an assumption?

It's certainly not the way I respond to the world's historical past and I doubt it's the way you do either. I don't look at the Pharaohs and go: "Well the Egyptians were a bit dark so I'm not interested in their stupid pyramids"; I don't reject the achievements of the Chinese emperors because they were yellow, slanty-eyed, and couldn't speak a word of English. I see global history as everyone's history; I see all the amazing tales which have sprung during your nation's history and my nation's history as inspirational ones in which we can all share.

More important than that, I see our national stories—of King Alfred and George Washington; of Lord Nelson and Stephen Decatur; of Stanley and Livingstone; and of Lewis and Clark—as being vital to our countries' sense of unity, social cohesion, and selfhood. When a Somali or a Congolese or an Iraqi or a Bangladeshi refugee starts his new life in Britain, I want him to learn about the Battle of Hastings, and the Spanish Armada, and the Battle of Waterloo, and feel the same stirrings in his heart as if he'd been born an Englishman. And if he'd emigrated to the United States instead, I hope he'd come to feel exactly the same way about Thomas Jefferson and Alexander Hamilton, Robert E. Lee and Ulysses S. Grant, and Teddy Roosevelt's and the Rough Riders' charge up the Kettle and San Juan Hills.

Your naturalization process for new citizens currently has a huge advantage over ours because, being Americans, you're not burdened by that dreadful embarrassment and self-hatred which afflicts most Britons when they think of concepts like nationhood and patriotism. Unlike us, you're not afraid to make your would-be citizens swear an oath of allegiance to the flag as a condition of entry. In Britain, all that's required pretty much is that you answer twenty-four multiple choice questions on life in the United Kingdom ("Who is the Prime Minister? a) Ricky Gervais, b) Gordon Brown, c) Donald Duck") and not show up on police searches as a known terrorist. And even the second one isn't a complete no-no, if you've fled from a country where your life is deemed at risk. In this case, under EU Human Rights law, your right to be given asylum is deemed to trump the fear that you might be a mass-murderer intent on blowing up your new neighbors.

But if you're tempted to start feeling too smug and superior about this, don't be. With Obama at the helm and Democrats controlling both houses of Congress, you're going to see an explosion in just the kind of multiculturalism madness we in socialist Britain have been suffering for over a decade. Do you really think the Democrats will be tougher on illegal immigration than the Republicans were? Do you really think the Democrats will do more to encourage traditional patriotic education in your public school classrooms than the Republicans did? (And in both cases we know the Republicans did damn little.) And do you really think that your traditional Christmas cheer won't get further elbowed aside—as it has in Britain by the "winter lights festival"—by the "winter holidays," including made-up holidays like Kwanza, and that your kids will risk suspensions if they so much as give a Christmas card to a friend at school or sing a Christmas carol on the playground or wear a crucifix necklace at Easter?

Demands for apologies and reparations for the crimes of the slave trade will grow ever shriller; the cult of ethnicity—already so well-entrenched in your seats of learning thanks the black and gender studies departments—will become more widespread; the achievements of great Americans (especially dead white male Americans) will be denigrated; America's national culture will be downgraded and those of other cultures, particularly non-Western ones, will be exalted.

You'll hear plenty about white guilt. But very little about William Wilberforce, the British Tory MP who led the campaign to abolish the slave trade or the Royal Navy that put a stop to it. And even less about the Ashanti tribespeople who profited as much from the trade as any white man. (And who are in fact quietly proud of it. There's a hand shake they all do in Ghana which involves feeling your way to one another's pinkies, grasping the top joint, and then releasing it with a satisfying click. This is the joint that slave masters would traditionally chop off to mark their property. In other words, the Ghanaian handshake is saying: "We are not slaves!" Delightful people. Great country. Well worth a visit.)

Nowhere will this battle for the soul of America—for that it is what it is—prove more fraught and vicious than in the field of immigration. Once again, we unfortunates in Britain are ahead of the curve on this one. In the last decade, our country has been changed immeasurably and mostly for the worse—with our social services and transport systems overwhelmed, our traditions eroded, our national character diluted, our culture threatened— by the greatest wave of immigration since our history began.

Net immigration to Britain is running at nearly 350,000 a year, with immigrants now accounting for 83 percent of all new population growth. By American standards this may not seem much but Britain is a much smaller country with a population density twelve times greater than yours (and four times denser than France's and twice as dense as Germany's). By 2031—and this is an official government estimate, so most likely on the low side— our population is expected to have swollen by another 6 million: this on a crowded island where the transport infrastructure's collapsing, our roads are maddeningly congested, the schools have no more spaces, and the hospital waiting lists are already stretching round the block.

Why is no one complaining about this? Well, they are. Just beginning to. But for years no one did, first because the Labour government kept the scale of immigration a secret—through a "don't ask, don't tell" policy of refusing to measure it—and second because of the speech we mentioned earlier. The one almost everyone agreed with but which wasn't open for discussion because the PC control freaks in government decided they knew better.

And this is by no means a purely "racist" white complaint. In Britain, certainly, among the most fervent anti-immigrant out-pourings I've heard were from the Bangladeshi couple who used to run my local corner shop, and from an old Jamaican man who'd been part of the first wave of West Indians to arrive here in the late 1940s. In both cases their complaint was exactly the same: "These incomers, they have no respect for our culture. They just don't understand the old ways."

Indeed *they* don't. Thanks to the disastrous, heavily entrenched policy of multiculturalism—to be discussed further in the next chapter—new immigrants to Britain have little or no incentive to assimilate into the prevailing culture. Au contraire: their "differ-ence" and their "diversity" are considered special, cherishable qualities which we must all "celebrate," regardless of the costs this may have to social cohesion.

For the Ugandan Asians who fled to Britain from Idi Amin's terror in the 1970s, for the West Indians who came over in the 1950s, for the Greeks and Turks who sought refuge from the trou-bles afflicting Cyprus, for those whose Jewish ancestors fled the Polish pogroms of the 1890s, for descendants of the Huguenots who fled persecution in France in the seventeenth and eighteenth centuries as much as for people whose English ancestry predates the Norman Conquest, the problem is one and the same: the cul-ture of the land they love is vanishing before their eyes.

But am I perhaps not a little biased here in favour of the WASP status quo? Of course I am. I'm a white, Anglo Saxon, Church of England protestant, public-school and Oxford-educated. As Eng-lish as English could be. Well, and also a bit Welsh too. My mother's maiden name is Price, which is a corruption of the Welsh surname Ap Rhys (Son of Rhys), so somewhere down the line, I guess my ancestors would have been rustling sheep, and hiding in caves like Prince Llewellyn did before the blacksmith betrayed him to the English and he was hanged, drawn, and quartered. Then, come the Industrial Revolution, my Welsh peasant forebears would have abandoned the land and gravitated towards the big English cities, where all the jobs were. They would have lost their Welsh accents, abandoned their heritage, and assimilated so thoroughly that by the generation when my maternal grandmother married my maternal grandfather Price she would have had no idea whatsoever that she was marrying into a Welsh bloodline. And nor, funnily enough, would he.

God knows where the name Delingpole comes from. In my more optimistic moments I like to imagine its either Huguenot French, or better still, a corruption of De La Pole. The De La Poles were the Earls of Lincoln and Suffolk in the fourteenth century. There was also a Welsh prince called Owain De La Pole. But obviously a chap with an ego like mine is going to be drawn to the idea of having aristocratic ancestry. Probably, though, I'm desperately ordinary and even my name isn't that special. Just a clerical error by someone who mistranscribed some boring name like Dillyfield. Which means that the only thing of note any known ancestor of mine ever did was invent a fire escape. It was a ladder with a canvas chute underneath so that if you were unable to climb down you could slide down instead. His name was Abraham Wivell. He's in the London Science Museum, or used to be.

On my wife's side of the family things are a bit more exotic. Her late mother was Anglo-Welsh upper class. Her father—my children's grandfather—is one quarter Italian and three quarters Bulgarian. His surname is Daneff and two of his ancestors were Prime Ministers of Bulgaria. During the war, his homeland was allied with the Germans, bombed by the Allies, and occupied by the Soviets, so he fled first to Constantinople and later to England where he was raised by his elder sister and schooled in the English way.

Meeting him now you'd never guess he was other than thoroughly British. Till maybe you got talking to him about politics and discovered how deeply he loathes Communists—they took his ancestral estates and kept much of his family imprisoned behind the Iron Curtain. As a journalist in the 1950s and 1960s his specialty was reporting on the Eastern Bloc and one of his friends—Georgi Markov—was notoriously assassinated by the Bulgarian intelligence services with a poisoned umbrella. These aren't the kind of experiences which leave much room for left-wing idealism.

My family's history then, is a story of migration and assimilation. No big deal there: so are ALL our family histories, yours probably more so than mine being as you're from the land of *E Pluribus Unum*. Our societies are all the better for it, I'm sure, and our gene pools the stronger for it. But the fact that this is so scarcely constitutes an argument for unfettered immigration in the future.

When the shocking scale of immigration to the UK was first publicized a few years ago by an enterprising private organization called MigrationWatch, the immediate response from the liberal-left—together with all the usual arguments about the supposed economic benefits—was that Britain was a "mongrel nation" which could absorb the new wave of immigrants as easily it has had absorbed successive waves of Romans, Angles, Saxons, Jutes, and Danes.

Just the same arguments are used in the United States. "Don't you worry your pretty head about Open Borders," the fashionable line goes. "Never mind the fact that half of all migrants into the United States are Latin Americans, that by 2040 non-Hispanic whites will be a minority of all Americans, that by 2050 Hispanics may constitute 25 percent of America's population. It's all okay because it's the American way. First came the Protestant settlers; then the Germans, the Irish, the Scandinavians, the Eastern European Jews, the Italians. And let's never forget the Africans imported as slaves. And the Native Americans who were here before anyone. *E Pluribus Unum*—and proud!"

Which is all perfectly true up to a point, but what this argument ignores both in Britain and the United States is the issue of scale. As Samuel Huntington wrote of contemporary Hispanic immigration to the United States in his book *Who Are We?* "[Its] extent and nature differ fundamentally from those of previous immigration, and the assimilation successes of the past are unlikely to be duplicated with the contemporary flood of immigrants from Latin America. This reality poses a fundamental question: will the United States remain a country with a single national language and a core Anglo-Protestant culture? By ignoring this question, Americans acquiesce to their eventual transformation into two peoples with two cultures (Anglo and Hispanic) and two languages (English and Spanish)."

Huntington is right. We ARE ignoring this question. We are ignoring it for a number of reasons—some of them creditable, others rather less so.

You could argue, for example, that the draconian measures you'd need to stop the flow of Mexican immigration would contravene the spirit of the Land of the Free. I sympathize with this line. There's probably much truth in it. America is a big, open-hearted country, not a nasty, mean-spirited one. This may well make its browning—or rather its Hispanicizing—inevitable.

Or you could argue—as Michael Moore and all his *bien-pensant* chums no doubt would—that mass Hispanic immigration is about the best thing that could ever possibly happen to sissy, uptight WASP-ish America and that therefore nothing needs to be done to check it because it's great. I don't agree, but it is a position.

But what I think is totally and utterly reprehensible is the current complete non-argument which is mostly taking place, namely:

"Gee it's just too uncomfortable to talk about. Maybe if we ignore it long enough it will all go away. Or at least it'll be our kids' and our grandchildrens' problem, not ours."

I hate it not just because it's so cowardly but because it does all the liberal-left's work for it. The reason there is no full, honest debate about immigration is because the liberal-left has made it its business to see there is no full and honest debate. As they did with Enoch Powell forty years ago, so the *bien-pensants* continue to do today: to engineer a social and political climate where race is an issue quite beyond civilized discussion. Think about that, my American friends, next time you tip toe round the subject: you're acting as the personal Dobby the House Elf, bashing your own head, for the benefit of Jesse Jackson, Michael Moore, and ethnic client-state politics of the Democratic Party.

Me, I'm completely biased as you know, but I think there's a lot to be said for the argument that American culture is essentially WASP culture. This was something Richard Brookhiser bravely addressed in his 1991 book *The Way of the WASP*. In it he identified six related values or traits which he believed have made America what it is.

They are: Civic-mindedness ("the operation of conscience in social relations") which leads in turn to Industry which results in Success. Then there is Use (asking what things are good for: Utilitarian practicality) and Anti-sensuality (which has less to do with prudery than with judging pleasures according to Use—whether or not they're "good for you"). Finally, dominating and informing all the above, there is Conscience ("the inner light that shows us self-evident truths. . . . the source of whatever freedoms WASP society enjoys").

You might quibble with the details, but Brookhiser's analysis strikes me as an essentially fair one. We can all agree that in a pluralist society there must be a degree of tolerance for other values and traditions. But if we want our countries, Britain and America, to retain the characteristics that have made them great, we must surely accept that our core culture—our *Leitkultur*—is the WASP culture of our forefathers.

Is this an unhealthy or even a wrong thing to believe? There are many on the liberal-left who would have us think so. They're wrong, of course, and to see why they are wrong, you only have to ask a question Samuel Huntington asks in *Who Are We?* "Would the United States be the country that it has been and that it largely remains today if it had been settled in the 17th and 18th centuries not by British Protestants but by French, Spanish, or Portuguese Catholics? The answer is clearly no. It would not be the United States; it would be Quebec, Mexico, or Brazil."

Speaking for myself I feel uncomfortable with the slow homogenization of global culture. I'm not altogether convinced that much can be done about it and as a citizen of one of the world's most culturally diverse cities, I'm certainly more than used to it. But the small "c" conservative part of me rather likes the United States being itself and Quebec, Mexico, and Brazil being themselves; and it likes being able to wander through picturesque Yorkshire villages and see only white faces, and picturesque Ethiopian villages and see only black ones. Unlike Michael Moore and his mob, I don't hate my world so much that I particularly want to change it. I'm a conservative and I like things as they are.

But unlike some conservatives, I do recognize that there's no such thing in this debate as a neutral position. Staying neutral—or silent—isn't being neutral. It's participating in the great white liberal death wish.

Chapter Nine

DESTRUCTIVE DIVERSITY

DAUGHTERS: AREN'T THEY GREAT? If you haven't got one, I seriously recommend you try getting one. Especially, if you're a Dad. The Mom/daughter deal I'm not so sure about: they seem to understand one another's weaknesses too well. But the Dad/daughter relationship is one of the best things ever invented.

She thinks you're the handsomest, cleverest, wisest, funniest, most fantastically perfect man the world has known (unfortunately sowing the seeds for eternal disappointment with every boy she meets thereafter). You, in turn, as Dad, know that you are unreservedly beloved by the prettiest, brightest, most delectably charming, and boundlessly talented female in all creation. It's a match made in heaven, better even than marriage, because the purity of your love isn't sullied by the grubby complications of carnal desire.

This is why, whenever I can spare the time off work, I love to go with my daughter—Girl, 8—on the forty-minute journey by foot and public transport to her Church of England state primary school in Central London.

As we walk to the bus stop, hand in hand, Girl will chatter away to me about which of her best friends she currently adores, which of her best friends she SO hates and never liked at all because she's SO horrible, what she's studying in school, which songs she likes, what she's looking forward to doing this afternoon, where she wants to go next on holiday and so on, and I'll just listen, beaming.

"Did you learn anything from your daughter, today?" my wife will ask me later.

"Oh. This and that," I'll reply vaguely, because the truth is I won't have taken in a single word of what my daughter said. It's what goes with the territory of being a Dad. The sound of your daughter speaking is like a song of the Sirens: so mesmerisingly beautiful there's just no need to decipher the lyrics.

(So remember that next time, girls. It's not that we're sexist pigs who don't value your opinions. We're just too enchanted by your loveliness to take them in, that's all.)

Then we get to the bus stop, Girl and me, and our journey will take a more sinister turn. They're never a particularly pleasant experience, London buses at rush hour, for they're usually far too crowded with nowhere to sit (if you've been lucky enough to get on in the first place—sometimes you have to wait half an hour, while four or five full ones trundle frustratingly by), they're swarming with gangs of unruly, aggressive school kids (whom no one dares antagonize for fear of being stuck with a knife), and because, of course, there's always the possibility that this could be the journey where you and your daughter end up being blown to smithereens by an Islamist suicide bomber.

Not nice, huh?

I read a brilliant book just recently, by a journalist called Kevin Myers, who witnessed the very worst of "the Troubles" in Northern Ireland during the 1970s and 1980s. The passage which stuck in my mind is his description of what happened when he witnessed his first bomb. All around, he noticed, the ground was strewn what looked like pink rose petals. On closer examination, these turned out to be shards of human flesh.

I like my daughter as she is. I don't want her to be transformed—is this what Yeats meant when he wrote "A terrible beauty is born"?—into ten thousand and one pink rose petals. I don't want the pressure of the explosion to cause the tiny air pockets between her joints to expand so that her skeletal system collapses like a rag doll. I don't want the screws, and coins, and ball bearings, and bits of glass and springs, and all the other foul shrapnel with which the suicide bomber has stuffed his rucksack, tearing into my daughter's perfect soft skin, ripping out her beautiful blue eyes, penetrating the throat that has sung me so many beautiful songs, and obliterating the brain I'd always imagined was going to help her achieve so much, because she reads so well, and learns her piano and recorder so diligently, and delights me with so many clever, sassy, grown-up remarks about the glorious future she has planned for herself as a pop star, a dancer, a golf pro, an artist, and mother of all the kids whose diapers she's going to insist I change.

And I'm sorry if this is the kind of grisly detail you really don't want to read. But I think we need to recognize exactly what we're up against here. Unless we keep reminding ourselves—reminding ourselves till we're sick—of the grotesque physical reality of the threat posed by the ideology which seeks to destroy us and our civilization, we will be well over half way to surrendering to it.

We need to imagine how it must have been for all the passengers on Flight 93 when, knowing the fate that awaited them, they made those final, tearful cell phone calls to their loved ones.

We need to empathise with the gnawing anxiety experienced daily by Jerusalem bus-passengers and London underground commuters, as they wonder: "Is this going to be the day when the last words I ever hear are the crazy with the beard and the suicide vest hurling himself towards his 72 virgins with a final 'Allahu Akhbar!'?" We need to recall in minute detail the horror of what happened in New York and Washington, D.C., on 9/11, in London on 7/7, in Madrid on those commuter trains, in Bali in those nightclubs. Because, if we don't, we end up with crap like this:

"As long as young people feel they have got no hope but to blow themselves up you are never going to make progress." That's Tony Blair's wife Cherie—a human rights lawyer—expressing at a Palestinian charity event what sounds suspiciously like veiled sympathy for suicide bombers.

"I think if I had to live in that situation—and I say that advisedly—I might just consider becoming one myself." That's former British Liberal Democrat MP Jenny Tonge—since promoted to the House of Lords as Baroness Tonge—expressing solidarity with suicide bombers after a trip to Palestine.

"America needs to ask itself why it's so hated." That's every other liberal newspaper editorial line in the aftermath of 9/11.

"If the United States is justified in launching a pre-emptive attack on Iraq, why then any nuclear power is justified in carrying out a pre-emptive attack on any other." That's Arundhati Roy, activist, thinker, author of your favorite unreadable Indian novel *The Goddess of Small Things*.

"Looks like what's happening is some sort of silent genocide." That's Noam Chomsky, the Left's favorite intellectual and America-hater, demonstrating with characteristic subtlety and insight why American intervention to overthrow a despotic woman-hating, homosexual-murdering, terrorism-supporting regime in Afghanistan is infinitely more culpable than the premeditated murder of 2,974 innocent civilians.

Something I've noticed about terrorist atrocities is how frighteningly quickly the public mood shifts: from unity to division, from resolve to equivocation, from urgency to complacency, from determination to resignation, from appalled horror to shoulder-shrugging acceptance.

Remember how scary it used to feel, catching an airplane in the first weeks and months after 9/11? You'd look at the lengthening lines brought about by all the extra security measures and almost rejoice at the inconvenience: "If it's a choice between early death and a longer wait, give me that extra hour's hassle, any day." You'd eye up all those of your fellow passengers with a vaguely Middle Eastern countenance, thinking: "Is that the one who's going to blow us all up? Or that one? Or that one? Or that one?" And when you got to your destination, through immigration and customs, and safely outside, you'd breathe a sigh worthy of a U.S. infantryman passing the final German bunker atop Omaha Beach. "I made it. I'm alive!" you'd think, a little hysterically perhaps but totally understandably. In those early days it felt like the terrorists were everywhere. If they didn't get you it was a minor miracle.

It was like that in London for a period after 7 July 2005— known thereafter as 7/7—when four young Islamists blew themselves up on crowded public transport (three of them on tube trains, one on a bus) killing fifty-two of their fellow passengers and injuring more than 700 others. You just knew that everyone in the not-nearly-so-crowded-as-usual tube carriages and buses was thinking the same thing as you: "The sooner I finish this journey the happier I'll be."

Just as World War II bomber pilots would instinctively, repeatedly sweep the skies for enemy fighter aircraft with a 360 degree roll of their eyes, so you would sweep your carriage for potential terrorists: first, as you entered; then with each subsequent stop as more passengers got on. And if you didn't like the look of anyone you weren't taking any chances. I remember once being on a tube train when a young guy with a beard and a slight suntan—student traveller probably—entered the carriage with a rucksack on his back. Before the doors had time to close behind him, a burly Australian commuter gently but firmly bustled him out of the train and back on the platform. "Sorry mate. Not in here you don't," the Aussie murmured. And the whole carriage cheered.

"Poor guy," part of me thought as I watched the bearded student standing disbelievingly on the platform. It must be so horrible when, through no fault of your own, you've become the victim of lynch-mob hysteria. Like Cinna the poet who gets stabbed to death by the vengeful crowd in *Julius Caesar* just because he happens to share a name with one of the conspirators; or the paediatric doctor in Wales who—at the height of one of Britain's regular child abuse scares—had his front door sprayed with the words "PAEDO SCUM" by someone who didn't know the difference between a paediatrician and a paedophile. "Then again," I thought, "pretty insensitive to come walking on a tube train looking like that at a time like this."

But almost worse than that lynch-mob hysteria is the false sense of security that follows. Sure it's a relief no longer feeling you have to poop your pants every time you use public transport; sure, it reflects well on the endurance of the human spirit, this London-Blitz-style determination to get on with your life and live it as normal and not let the enemy grind you down. Problem is, this flush of physical courage is all too often accompanied by an influx of moral cowardice and intellectual decadence.

The train of thought goes something like this: "Whew. This is nice! We haven't been blown to pieces for ages so things must be back to normal. Probably the security services are doing a smash-up job. Or maybe the threat was never as dire and widespread as it was cracked up to be. Or maybe with a black guy in the White House the Islamists have decided that from now on it's peace, brotherhood, and unity for all mankind. Whatever, I'm enjoying this, so let's not rock the boat. Let's do whatever we can to keep the Islamists happy."

And I totally understand this impulse, don't you? Saving your skin at almost any cost—it's what we're biologically programmed to do. I remember, with a twinge of guilt and self-disgust, what my most immediate response to 9/11 was. After I'd watched, open-mouthed, as that first plane smacked into the first tower, twigged what was happening and realized our world would never be the same again, I thought: "Look guys, if this is about Israel— *have* Israel." (And you're reading someone generally so philo-Semitic and pro-Zionist he makes Moshe Dayan look like Yasser Arafat.)

It completely ruined my cosy illusions of how I would have behaved under Nazi occupation, let me tell you. In my fantasy, I always used to be the one with the family of Jews hidden in my partition walls. But if my disgraceful 9/11 response was anything to go by, it would have been more like: "The Himmelfarbs, Herr Obersturmbannführer? Hidden door, behind the coal pile in the cellar at number 11."

At least in my case, though, this sordid impulse lasted but a moment. For many of my countryman, however, for large swathes of Europe, and for huge chunks of liberal America it has unfortunately become an article of faith that this really is the only sensible solution: "Give the enemy what they want and eventually they'll go away."

Britain has a fine and ancient tradition of this. In the old days it was called Danegeld—the protection money paid by the Anglo-Saxons to the Vikings in order not to be raped, pillaged, or spread-eagled (a particularly nasty Viking trick where they'd slice you down the middle of your chest, pull your rib cage apart so that you looked like, well, a spread eagle). Often the protection money wasn't quite enough, so after their payoff, the Vikings would come to do their raping, pillaging, and spread-eagling anyway. This they continued to do until King Alfred decided enough was enough and united his people to defeat the common threat. It worked. If it hadn't I suppose you'd be reading this in Norwegian.

More recently, in the years leading up to World War II we had something called the Appeasement movement. This derived from the cute, popular notion that despite one or two dubious quirks— the funny moustache, the vegetarianism, the hatred of fox-hunting, the expressed desire to destroy all the world's Bolshevik-Jewish-Slavic *untermenschen*, the evident lunacy—Adolf Hitler was nonetheless the sort of fellow with whom a chap could do business. What we needed to do was to feel his pain. Of course he was angry and embittered because of the terrible injustice inflicted on his country by the terms of the horrid Versailles treaty. So what better way to soothe his troubled spirit than by allowing him the odd *lebensraum*-gaining *Anschluss* here, the odd annexation of the Sudetenland there. And if that still didn't work, well, does any of us really care that much about quarrels in "a far away country between people of whom we know nothing?" (Which is how the appeaser's leader, Prime Minister Neville Chamberlain, character-ized Nazi Germany's plans to invade Czechoslovakia.)

In the end it all comes down to one simple question: is my cul-ture worth defending? If it isn't, then bring on the Vikings and the Nazis. If it is, then you'd better be ready to fight for it. Not just on a military level but—perhaps more important, because the terms of engagement are less obvious and the enemy's potential routes to victory more protean and insidious—the cultural one too.

Let's talk about multiculturalism: the philosophy of self-hating defeatism. I'm not sure who invented the concept. It just seems to have rolled in out of nowhere like some noxious miasma from a Stephen King novel and taken over most of the Western World. (Unless, did we maybe build our society on top of an ancient

Indian burial ground? Will we never learn?) But whoever was responsible deserves credit for at least one thing.

The name. Isn't it just pure genius? I mean, short maybe of "Serendipity" or "Incredibleorgasm" or perhaps "Limitlessrichesforeveryone," it's hard to think of a word more heartily guaranteed to win widespread and unquestioning popular support.

Multiculturalism. Mmm. Nice. So that must mean: ebony and ivory living together in perfect harmony; Thai green chicken curry and Bortsch and Spaghetti alla vongole and fajitas and falafels on our doorsteps; thrilling musical cross-pollinations like drum 'n' bass and dub and Afrobeat bluegrass bhangra, which doesn't exist yet but surely will one day; urgent new, prize-winning novels from Bombay and Lagos; *The Cosby Show*; Condoleeza Rice and Colin Powell. . . ?

Wrong. Multiculturalism is the very opposite of the "melting pot" philosophy which tries to bring people of all races and backgrounds together. It's about dragging them apart by emphasising their difference. About "celebrating diversity."

Celebrating diversity, like multiculturalism, is one of those weaselly forms of Orwellian Newspeak designed to make an intrinsically poisonous idea seem friendly and beneficial. It was popularised in Britain some time in the 1970s by a champagne socialist politician named Roy Jenkins, who suffered from a charming Elmer Fudd style speech defect (so really, he would have said "Cewebwate Diversity") but a much less charming, left-liberal intellectual defect, namely: a tragic inability to understand why his nation's culture was worth defending.

Jenkins—later ennobled Lord Jenkins, because we celebrate not just diversity in Britain, but idiocy too—was, like many of multiculturalism's champions, a learned and civilized man. The son of a coal-miner and union leader who had wrongly been imprisoned during the 1926 General Strike, young Roy won a scholarship to Oxford and took a first class honors degree before entering politics. A connoisseur of fine living (especially claret), he wrote nineteen books including much acclaimed biographies of British prime ministers William Gladstone and Winston Churchill.

You'd think that having enjoyed an education and career so steeped in the best of British tradition, Jenkins might have had an interest in standing up for the culture that created it. Not so. True to that self-hating instinct that afflicts so many liberals, Jenkins saw the blessings he had enjoyed not as a cause for celebration (sorry, cewebwation) but as reason for hand-wringing and guilt. If he had enjoyed all these benefits, why shouldn't everybody else in the world too? Why, more to the point, should British culture—essentially the creation of the white educated middle class and the aristocracy—be "privileged" to the detriment of other cultures? Wasn't this precisely the kind of elitist attitude that progressives like Jenkins ought to be setting an example by trying to stamp out?

And so it was that a philosophy born of white-liberal guilt and devised with (groan!) the noblest of intentions was soon seized upon by Marxist agitators, town hall Trotskyites, and minority-rights grievance mongers, to lend intellectual weight to their ongoing plan to destroy the Establishment and overthrow "The System."

Soon the multicultural virus had spread through our schools, our universities, through local government, through our hospitals, through the BBC, leaving almost no area of British life unaffected.

I have on my desk in front of me just one tedious example. It is a leaflet from my daughter's school, asking me—on behalf of the Department for Education and Skills—to identify her ethnic background. Is she: White British; Irish; Traveller of Irish Heritage; Gypsy/Roma; Albanian; Portuguese; Kosovan; White Eastern European; White Western European; or White of Other Background? Or is she: Mixed white and black Caribbean; white and black African; white and Asian; or other Mixed background? Or is she: Indian; Pakistani; Bangladeshi; or from another Asian background? Or is she black and Caribbean; or African; or Angolan; or Congolese or Ghanaian; or Nigerian or Sierra Leonean; or Somalian or Sudanese; or from another black background? Or is she Chinese? Or is she from any other ethnic background, namely, Afghan, Arab Other, Egyptian, Iranian, Iraqi, Kurdish, Lebanese, Libyan, Moroccan, Yemeni, or any other ethnic background?

Someone out there is being paid to collate this information. Being government employees, they're also being provided with healthcare and a guaranteed pension. Trees have been chopped down and government-favored printing firms paid large sums to print the leaflet. Translators have been employed to add, in thirteen different languages, a note inviting parents who don't understand English to apply for a request form which translates the full document into their own language.

Where's the money for all this coming from? Me. The taxpayer.

And my reward for all this as the guy who's paying for it would be, er, what exactly? Where's the benefit to any of that rainbow nation of kids in my daughter's classroom? Suppose, after much expensive research, it emerges that maybe the Congolese boy belongs to a group statistically less likely to do well at Math or Roma kids find it difficult to stay still in one spot for very long. What's the government going to do? Spend yet more of my money on extra tuition for preferred minorities, making the kids in question feel weird and different when surely all they want is to be made to feel like any other kid. Like they're normal. Like they belong.

It's not the expense or the bureaucracy or the time wasting or the flabbergasting pointlessness I most object to about the multiculturalist project, though. It's the almost incalculable damage it does to social cohesion.

The more you urge incomers to emphasise their differences from the prevailing cultural norms, the less reason you give them to assimilate. I hardly need to preach to Americans about the dangers of the ghetto mentality to which this leads. I saw it for myself (quite by accident, on holiday actually) during the Los Angeles riots while driving with a journalist colleague through South Central in a red convertible sports car. It wasn't the most understated mode of transport from which to witness some of the worst civil unrest in twentieth century American history, but my colleague had come straight from San Diego where he'd been covering the America's Cup. To this day, I'm sure the only reason we didn't get ourselves shot was because none of the heavily armed blacks and Hispanics we saw cruising in their pick ups either side of us could quite believe two white guys could be so dumb.

But if you want to see the effects of multiculturalism at their most extreme and damaging, come to Britain. Come sit next to my daughter and me on that scary bus journey. And ask yourself why it is that the guy standing opposite—British-born, British-educated, with an unmistakeable British accent and a favorite British football team—yet believes that he's our enemy and that he must kill us.

Apart from the Islam stuff, I mean.

Not, obviously, that I'm seeking to downplay the jihadist propaganda which has brought our bearded chum to this dramatic pass. Of course he's doing it because he thinks this is what's demanded in the Koran, because he thinks it's what Allah wants. But what I'm asking here is: "Why isn't he more immune to this bullshit? Why does he feel more loyalty to the Ummah—the Muslim diaspora—than he does to the land of his birth? Why does he not feel as British as all the other Brits he's trying to kill?"

In a word: multiculturalism.

After the 7/7 suicide bombings many commentators in the liberal media expressed surprise that they were carried out not by the evil agents of some foreign regime, but by apparently law-abiding, peace-loving British citizens. How, they wondered, had Britain become so divided; so Balkanized?

Maybe they should have asked Ray Honeyford, the school-teacher from Bradford, in the North of England, who was hounded out of his job by their liberal media forebears in the early 1980s. His crime? To have written a magazine article expressing his concern that Multiculturalism was creating irreparable divisions among British schoolchildren; that "diversity" was a disaster waiting to happen.

Bradford is a once-prosperous wool-manufacturing town, now segregated on lines as ruthlessly demarcated as any in Apartheid-era South Africa. One side of the main road is white working class; the other is an outpost of Islam where there is not a white face to be seen. The British writer Theodore Dalrymple once brilliantly anatomised the scene thus in *City Journal*: "It is strictly men only on the street, dressed as for the North-West Frontier (apart, incongruously, from their sneakers); a group of them perpetually mills around outside the house that functions as a madrassa, or Muslim school. Horace's famous line of two millennia ago comes to mind: they change their skies, not their souls, who run across the sea."

These divisions were evident, even in the early 1980s, but Ray Honeyford—then headmaster of a middle school in Bradford's immigrant area—believed they were not irreparable. To stop the rot, though, he argued in the magazine *The Salisbury Review*, the authorities must first recognize the fatal contradictions inherent in multiculturalism. The way, for example, in the supposed interests of social justice multiculturalism's champions pretended that racism in Britain was purely a white phenomenon (despite widespread evidence of African v. West Indian, Muslim v. Sikh, violence); and the way it chose to ignore the misery Muslims inflicted on women, in what was supposed to be a post-feminist society, through arranged marriages and even honor killings.

Of particular concern to Honeyford as a responsible headmaster was the way many of his Muslim parents would send their children back to Pakistan or Bangladesh for months or even years at a time, often as a deliberate measure to prevent them from acquiring British cultural characteristics. Under British law a parent is obliged, once his child is registered with a school, to ensure his regular attendance. Were any of his white parents to flout this obligation, he pointed out, they would undoubtedly be punished. Yet in the case of Muslim parents, the local authorities were prepared to turn a blind eye. This, said Honeyford, was a "blatant and officially sanctioned policy of racial discrimination."

In the furore that followed—whipped up by local newspapers, "anti-racist" pressure groups, and catch-vote politicians—Honeyford received death threats, was besieged by mobs chanting "Raycist" and repeatedly vilified in the liberal media. Though teaching was his love, he reluctantly took early retirement to spare himself, his wife, and his school further intrusion.

One quarter of a century on, none of the problems Honeyford so courageously raised has been addressed and many of the disasters he predicted have come to pass. In towns which, besides Bradford, include Beeston, Dudley, and Luton, as well as large swathes of cities like London and Birmingham, there now exist Muslim ghettoes in almost total isolation from the traditional cultural life of Britain. They have their own dress-style (Pakistani-style salwar kameez; the Hijab; sometimes even the full, Taliban-approved Burka); their own legal system (the Sharia, currently only used for civil matters, though Islamist campaigners are pushing for it to be extended); and, increasingly, their own faith schools.

"And where's the harm in that?"your cultural relativist might argue. "Is that really so different from the Amish? From Christians and their faith schools?" Hmmm. Well I can think of at least one difference. As far as I know Christian and Amish schools don't teach their children that people of other faiths—"those whom God has cursed and with whom he is angry"—are "monkeys" and "pigs." Nor do they set their kids classroom tasks in which they have to list "repugnant" characteristics of the Jews.

Yet this, it emerged in an industrial tribunal, was what pupils were being taught at one London Islamic school, co-funded by the UK taxpayer and the Saudi government.

Church of England Schools, I know, because my daughter goes to one will always—in their typically accommodating tea-sipping, biscuit-munching Anglican way—bend over backwards to say kindly things about rival religions. Which is why I find it so maddening when leftist political commentators demand the banning of all kinds of faith school on the grounds that somehow they're equally responsible for fomenting intolerance and division. No they're not. Only one faith is, and you guys are just too cowardly to name it.

Indeed the pusillanimity of the liberal establishment generally in Britain towards this enemy within has been quite breathtaking. Consider the Bishop of Oxford, who urged his parishioners to welcome controversial plans for amplified calls-to-prayer to be broadcast from a mosque in central Oxford. Never mind that this is supposed to be the city of "dreaming spires" rather than "wailing minarets." Said the bishop: "I think part of living in a tolerant society is saying: 'I don't agree with this but I accept it as part of my responsibility of being part of a diverse community.' "

Consider the response of the West Midlands Police to an undercover investigation by a Channel 4 documentary film crew into extremist preaching by radical imams at British mosques. One cleric was secretly filmed saying that the killer of a British soldier in Afghanistan was a "hero of Islam"; others were shown saying that "Allah created the woman deficient," that homosexuals should be thrown off mountains, and that young girls should be hit if they do not wear the hijab. Did the police prosecute any of these imams, as they were entitled to do under new legislation designed to curb "incitement to hatred"? Why no. Instead, they seized Channel 4's tapes and tried to prosecute the filmmaker for "misleading editing" which, they claimed—before the case was thrown out and Channel 4 won libel damages—ran the risk of stirring up racial hatred.

But my personal favorite example of abject cowardice in the face of the enemy—not to mention truly toe-curling disingenuousness—was in the first episode of a new BBC drama series called *Bonekickers*. Of which, more in a moment.

There may be some conservatives in the United States—though not many: not if they read Andrew Sullivan, Roger Kimball, or Mark Steyn—who still take the BBC at its own estimation of itself, as a *Masterpiece Theater* style guardian of the cultural flame and a bastion of integrity, authority, and balance. This has not, however, been the case for a long, long time. During the first Gulf War, it seemed at times so pro-Iraqi that wags christened it the Baghdad Broadcasting Corporation. On any given subject, the BBC's position is wearisomely predictable.

If it's covering the Middle East it will be bigging up the gallant Hezbollah freedom fighters and the plucky Palestinians at the expense of the sadistic, murdering, human-rights-trampling, homes-of-innocent-wailing-women-bulldozing, child-shooting, damn-near-as-bad-as-the-Nazis Israeli oppressors.

If it's covering the European Union, it will treat every politician who is not in favor of selling still more of Britain's rights down the river in the cause of "ever closer political union" as a rabid, swivel-eyed, crypto-fascist loon. Politicians who do believe in the Socialist European Superstate, on the other hand, are treated with deference a devout Catholic might accord the Pope. No, more than that, such as he might accord God.

If it's covering the environment it will, of course, believe everything that has ever been said by Greenpeace about polar bears, insist we're all doomed and that the only solution is to tax ourselves back to the Dark Ages.

If it's covering the Global Economic Meltdown, it will do so with an ever-so-slight smirk because it never did much believe in the Capitalist system and is quietly thrilled that Karl Marx may yet be proved right.

If it's covering any war in which the United States or Britain is involved, it will be of the view that the enemy are secretly the good guys and that, as imperialist aggressors, we thoroughly deserve to get our asses whupped.

If it's covering Islam, well . . . what do you think?

It got off to a great start quite early on in the war on terror with a three-part documentary series called *The Power of Nightmares.* This contrived to suggest that the global Islamist threat was largely a figment of our imagination—a "nightmare" which had been cynically conjured up by our governments to make us more scared, more keen to keep them in power, more accepting of their authoritarianism. Better still, it made out that Neoconservatives and Islamofascists are in fact soul-mates, both being motivated by fundamentalist religious zeal to destroy democratic society and rebuild it in their own image. Naturally, this *Fahrenheit 9,11* for pseudo-intellectuals was massively well-received by liberals every-where. The left-wing *Guardian* newspaper crowed: "This intelligent, scintillating series is a must for anyone who has the remotest interest in what is going on in the world."

But where self-hating, *bien-pensant,* surrender-monkeying lunacy was concerned, *The Power of Nightmares* was merely an *amuse gueule.* So too was the episode of the popular BBC spy series *Spooks* where the Middle Eastern hijackers who took over a London Embassy and began shooting hostages on the hour every hour turned out to be Jews in disguise. And so was the other *Spooks* episode where a group of suicidal religious extremists who launched grenade and bomb attacks on innocent members of another faith proved to be, yep, Christian fundamentalists.

It was *Bonekickers* that stole the crown. Though now widely hailed by connoisseurs of lame TV drama as among the risibly inept programmes in the history of broadcasting, *Bonekickers* was never designed that way. It was supposed to be huge. It was created by the writer/production team responsible for the hit time-travelling, retro-pastiche cop series *Life on Mars*; it had high production values; it had name-actors who'd appeared in classy Jane Austen dramas; it was about a team of groovy archaeologists (archaeology's BIG in Britain. It's how we pass the long winter nights: watching programs about men with beards and hard hats in trenches, digging); the faces were young, attractive, and multiracial (provoking guffaws in Britain's predominantly middle-aged, bearded, and extremely white archaeological community); there were lashings of ancient myth and hints of the supernatural. It was going to be *Indiana Jones* meets *The Da Vinci Code*. It was going to be...

Crap, as it turned out. The acting was wooden, the scripts were dire, the premises were risible, the climax scenes so hilariously bathetic they made your typical "If it hadn't been for those darned kids..." *Scooby Doo* pay-off look like *North by Northwest*. But all this most of us could forgive. Bad TV is not a crime. Bad TV is often good TV because it's so funny. What wasn't so funny was the story line in the first episode. The one where the archaeological team discover fragments of the True Cross, which quickly attracts the attention of a group of (white, Christian, it goes without saying) Knights Templars. These Knights Templars won't stop at anything in their burning desire to reignite the Crusades. So the first thing they do is capture a typically nice, reasonable, peace-loving young Muslim guy off the streets. And slice his head off.

Yeah I know, I know. Happens all the time doesn't it? Those pesky Christian fundamentalists and their endless decapitations of innocent Muslims. My fear is that they're just never going to be happy till they've restored the Caliphate, converted every infidel, and transformed the whole world into the Dar Al-Islam. No, wait. Hang on a second. That's the other guys, isn't it? Now I'm really confused.

The thing I don't understand about all this—that and the fact that only a 100 viewers rang to complain: then again, maybe BBC viewers are used to it by now—is what kind of mindset you'd need to write a storyline like that. I mean, I'm all for rooting for the underdog and a dose of bracing contrarianism. But doesn't there come a point where fear of upsetting a tiny minority of minority viewers and the understandable urge to brown-nose your commissioning editor by endorsing their PC values ought maybe to take second place to the slightly more important stuff? Stuff like, maybe, truth, reality, honesty, integrity, plausibility, social responsibility, and, er, NOT setting up a false moral equivalence between a religion whose members are all peaceful, law-abiding, and socially-integrated and one, at least some of whose members are extremely violent, dangerous, and given to cutting innocent victims' throats for the greater glory of Allah?

This is what I often think about when I'm on those bus trips to school with my beautiful Girl, always with that nagging worry at the back of my mind that this might be the last trip we ever take. I think: "If only it were all just a game. If only we lived in a world where theories had no consequences. Where doctrinaire lefties could experiment with all their delightful-sounding schemes to do with fairness and equality and multiculturalism and ethnic monitoring and positive discrimination and moral relativism while the rest of us got on with our lives completely unscathed."

Sometimes too I think, with a shudder, of something that happened a few weeks after 7/7 when another group of British-born Muslims tried to pull off a similar terrorist atrocity, also using rucksack bombs on buses. This time, fortunately, the bombs didn't go off—which meant that there were plenty of eyewitness accounts of how the would-be killers behaved.

The story that has always haunted me was the one told by the mother who was carrying a baby on the bus. One of the delusions you tend to suffer as a parent—I know I do—is to imagine that your children are so special and delightful that no sentient adult could ever possibly wish them harm. You imagine that were, say, a terrorist to be standing next to them on the bus with his bomb about to go off, he would look at your kids, see how pure and innocent and lovely they are, and either abort his mission or go to find some more suitable targets to kill.

This isn't what happens in real life, as the woman with the baby on the bus recounted. Shortly before the terrorist tried to detonate his bomb, he saw her, saw her baby, and turned his back so that his explosive rucksack was towards her. This is the real world. This is how it is. Such a pity that there are so many people out there who JUST DON'T GET IT.

Chapter Ten

GIVE WAR A CHANCE

HEY, HEY, CAPTAIN JACK
MEET ME DOWN BY THE RAILROAD TRACK
WITH MY RIFLE IN MY HAND
I'M GOING TO BE A SHOOTIN' MAN
A SHOOTIN' MAN
THE BEST I CAN
FOR UNCLE SAM.

My, what a damned fine marching song that is. A song as stir-ring as that and you can go for miles, barely feeling the weight of your M1 helmet, your M1 Garand, and the ammo in your web-bing as you trudge to the front through the biting wind and the Ardennes snow. Panzer divisions? Schmanzer divisions! They're no match for the might of the All-American Division!

Not that I was ever actually there you understand. I'm far too young to have fought in World War II and if I had I would have been fighting for the British. With the Long Range Desert Group, I like to think. Or maybe the Commandos. Or possibly as a Spitfire pilot. The fantasy changes by the day—and I do fantasize about it a lot. You could say I'm obsessed with war. I AM obsessed with war. I'm so obsessed with war I belong to a Facebook group called Obsessed with War and if you too are obsessed with war you might care to join. You'll like our group's motto. It's "All We Are Saying Is Give War a Chance."

This is how I know what it's like to march along with an M1 Garand singing that Captain Jack marching song. I recently joined a re-enactors' group which doubles as two U.S. wartime units— D Company 505th PIR, 82nd Airborne Division and C Company, 82nd Recon, 2nd Armored Division.

You'll notice that these are American outfits. It's not that I have anything against British army re-enactor groups—well apart from the scratchy, uncomfortable battledress and the fact that they don't have nearly so much armor. Just that my next novel is set during the Battle of the Bulge, which as you know was a mostly American affair.

My hero in the book is called Dick Coward—there's going to be a whole series of Dick Coward books, maybe ten in all—and I invented him to be a kind of anti-Flashman (if you haven't read the Flashman novels of George MacDonald Fraser, you should). Coward is a guy who everyone thinks is yellow (the name doesn't help) but who is really like most of us would be in a war, scared and reluctant to die, but nonetheless cheerfully willing to make the ultimate sacrifice if necessary for the sake of his buddies and the land he loves.

Though Dick is mostly upper class British, I've also made him part American—like Winston Churchill was. Partly this comes from my nakedly commercial desire to break into the American market. (You are SO going to love the thrilling scene where he crosses the river Waal with 504th PIR.) Less cynically, though, it's a reflection of my belief that our two great nations are never better than when fighting side by side in a common cause.

We're the good guys. We're the reason the world is in currently not nearly as bad a state as it would have been had we ducked our responsibilities and chosen not to do the right thing.

We did the right thing in the two World Wars. We did it in Korea. We're doing it now in Iraq and Afghanistan. And I don't think we pat ourselves on the back nearly often enough for the great things we've achieved and the great things we continue to achieve.

Let's say it again. We are the good guys. And let's keep saying it so we never forget it. The moment we start believing we're not the good guys—see the cultural and moral relativism we discussed earlier—is the moment our cause will be lost.

It is not my intention in this chapter to suggest that Democrats are useless at war. (Three letters would explode that argument: FDR).

Nor am I going to try arguing that socialists don't get the point of war. (Not, at least, if you believe the magnificent Christopher Hitchens is still a socialist, or that Adolf Hitler was.)

Nor yet am I going to predict that Obama's foreign policy will be a flop. (Who knows? Maybe Ahmadinejad really will cancel his entire nuclear weapons program because all he ever wanted was a United States president with the audacity to be hopeful).

I'm definitely, definitely not going to suggest that Republicans always get it right. (The Rumsfeld Doctrine? De-baathification? Paul Bremer?)

And I'm not going to deny that our nations' foreign policy should be open to scrutiny. Of course it should. Especially where military action is concerned and the lives of our boys and girls are at stake, it is clearly vital that we keep asking awkward questions about cost, effectiveness, and strategic objectives.

What I am going to argue, though, is this. War is hell but war is necessary. War will always be necessary. Conservatives understand this far better than liberals generally do and are thus, on the whole, better equipped to fight it and better equipped to win it. If you value national security, then you are better off under a conservative regime than you are under a liberal one.

Sometimes we forget this. Our enemies never do.

Consider Iran. After the Iranian Revolution in 1979, President Carter immediately recognized the new, avowedly anti-Western, anti-American Khomeini regime and offered to sell arms to it. Iran's response was to demand the return of the Shah, and when the United States didn't oblige the Iranians violated a centuries-old principle of international law by capturing fifty-two American diplomats and holding them hostage for 444 days. Within minutes of Ronald Reagan taking over the presidency, the Iranians very sensibly chose to release those hostages. They knew all too well what a Republican gunslinger would have done to them if they hadn't.

This example helps explode one of the great liberal myths about conservatives: that they are warmongers whose fetishizing of all things military inevitably leads to more wars.

In fact, quite the opposite is true. Suppose you're an Islamist, or a revolutionary Communist, or a Nazi: which kind of Western democracy are you most likely to challenge militarily? The one with the big stick it's prepared to use at a moment's notice? Or the one with the biggish stick it might or might not use, depending on how squeamish the administration feels about what a grisly, horrid business war is?

I have just been reading—as we war obsessives do—another book about Hitler. This one describes those key early moments when Hitler began expanding his evil empire, territory by territory: the Rhineland, Austria, the Sudetenland, the rest of Czechoslovakia, Poland. . . . What's fascinating is to realize how nervous this made his generals. Because of what happened later, we think of the Nazis as a ruthless, unstoppable war machine, united in their desire to conquer the world, fearless of all opposition. In fact, many of Hitler's senior officers were quietly appalled at the tempest this strange, angry man was preparing to reap for their beloved Germany. (They hadn't yet realized that *Götterdämmerung* was part of the game plan.) Foremost in their minds, as responsible strategists, was their anxiety about how the great powers Britain, France and, ultimately, the United States might respond to each increasingly provocative territorial incursion.

Hitler, however, knew better. He had seen clearly at the 1938 Munich conference—and guessed earlier—that the future Allied powers simply didn't have the stomach for war. Instead of conducting the messy battle his senior officers had feared against the Czech army's thirty-four divisions and the combined might of Britain and France, Hitler was able thanks to British and French appeasement at Munich to swallow up the whole of Czechoslovakia without a fight.

"Peace with honor" is how the British Prime Minister Neville Chamberlain described this shabby sacrifice. (He was a conservative, but of the wet-blanket school.) "An unmitigated defeat—the first sip of a bitter cup that will be proffered to us year by year—unless by a supreme effort of moral health and martial vigour, we arise again and take our stand for freedom," was Winston Churchill's more realistic assessment.

Churchill was, of course, vindicated in the end. But not before having undergone a long, miserable period of political isolation—he called it "The Wilderness Years"—in which he repeatedly warned of the dangers of German rearmament, only to be derided as a reactionary troublemaker who had failed to learn the lessons of the last world war.

What were these lessons? One, certainly, is that a protracted mechanized conflict which wipes out the flower of your nation's youth—885,000 in Britain, 1,397,800 in France, 116,700 in the United States—is a thing much to be feared and avoided. This "Never again" attitude explains why Chamberlain's appeasement policies found such widespread support, even as late as 1938, when anyone with eyes to see ought surely have been able to work out what Hitler's intentions were.

Appeasement has been justified since on the grounds of pragmatism: it bought breathing space for Britain to build up her military, especially her air force, after two decades of neglect. Sure this was part of the reason for it. What it owed rather more to, though, was the boundless human capacity for denying the inevitable. Nobody wanted war to happen. Therefore, if only they wished hard enough—or buried their heads in the sand deep enough—it *wouldn't* happen.

This denial technique didn't work. It never does in the face of a committed opponent hell-bent on your destruction, but you'd be amazed by how many are willing to give it a try. Even an operator as canny as Joe Stalin did, for a time. In 1939, he made his infamous non-aggression pact with Hitler which he genuinely, sincerely believed would spare the Soviet Union the immediate prospect of invasion by Nazi Germany. We know he did because in June 1941, even as the Nazi divisions gathered on his borders, and despite countless intelligence warnings from his spies, Stalin refused to allow his generals to mobilize his defenses—for fear of provoking his trusted ally. When one of his field marshals phoned to tell him the invasion had begun, Stalin was so shocked he couldn't speak.

Please excuse the retelling of stories you already know. My point is the fairly obvious one that he who ignores the lessons of history is condemned to repeat them. That point is obvious to conservatives who, being drawn to the past, understand this instinctively, but it's not so obvious to Liberals. For them, history is neither a source of comfort nor a route to greater understanding; only a nightmare from which they are trying to awake.

We saw some of this in Britain during the Blair regime. It wasn't just Labour that was now "New"—everything else had to be

New too, for these were the days of Cool Britannia (bigged up massively by its liberal cheerleaders in *Vanity Fair*), of pop stars like Noel Gallagher of Oasis coming for tea at 10 Downing Street, of a vacuous, all-consuming neophilia which would erase everything that was fusty and old and traditional and replace it with a shining New Jerusalem.

"Britain is a young country," Prime Minister Blair actually declared at one point. I said at the beginning he was a snake-oil salesman. Just how slippery a snake-oil salesman you'll see from the chutzpah of that statement, made without a flicker of self-doubt, or embarrassment, or concern that his nose might grow longer than Pinocchio's as he stood in the land of: Stonehenge; the Tower of London; the Sutton Hoo burial ship; King Arthur; Hadrian's Wall; Offa's Dyke; Boadicea; Julius Caesar; the Battle of Maldon; the Welsh Marches castles; the White Horse Of Uffington; Westminster Abbey; the Mappa Mundi; Tintern Abbey; the Domesday Book; Anne Hathaway's Cottage; Skara Brae; Lindisfarne; the Stone of Scone; Tintagel; Glastonbury Tor; the Wilton Diptych...

"How *does* the man get away with it?" some of us wondered, especially in those early days when Blair commanded the highest public approval ratings of any prime minister in history, dwarfing even those of Margaret Thatcher and Winston Churchill. Had the whole nation lost its head? And the answer was, yes, the whole nation had lost its head to this Belial-tongued Bambi, in much the same way that the nation lost its head when Princess Diana died in that Paris underpass in a car being driven too fast by a drunken French chauffeur.

I'll never forget where I was when I heard the news because it was the day after my wedding. I'd rung up my brother the morning after so he could give me the post-mortem on just what incredible fun our wedding reception had been and how happy he was for us. Instead he just said: "Princess Diana's died." I said:

"WHAT?" He said: "In a car crash." I said: "Blimey! That is weird beyond belief. Princess Diana? Dead? That's just impossible!"

Flashing back to the early 1980s, when the Prince of Wales first began courting Diana—then a nineteen-year-old aristocratic nursery schoolteacher, with a sweet face, a shy manner, and a slightly bobbly nose she'd later have seen to with plastic surgery—I remember saying to my brother: "Hey, bro. Have you seen the pictures of Charles's new girlfriend. What a fox, eh? Can you imagine someone as sexy as that being our Queen one day?" And my brother said: "It'll never happen. Babes as cute as that just don't get to be a Royal."

How prescient my brother was! (Though not for the reasons he thought.) Lady Diana Spencer duly married Prince Charles on a glorious sunny day on July 29, 1981, at a "fairy-tale wedding" watched by 750 million people around the world, including pretty much every household in Britain. Even many republican ones (republican, in the British sense: opposed to the monarchy, and in favour of a republic: in other words, lefties). For those who loathed the stuffiness and remoteness of monarchy, this coy, simpering, doe-eyed thing—who couldn't even get her husband's name right during the exchange vows at the altar—was surely the breath of fresh air which would sweep through the corridors of Buckingham Palace and teach those tight-arsed, stolid, hatchet-faced Windsors just what it is to be human.

We liked our Princess Di. Sure, we began slowly to discover over time that she was an arch-manipulator. And also a bit of a philanderer (but then again, so was her husband, who it seemed had never truly loved her and who started having affairs long before she did). But she was beguiling, she was great to look at in her succession of pretty outfits, she did good work for charity, and she made a wonderful ambassador for Britain, going round the world, looking foxy, flying the flag, being adored. She was our very own Jackie Kennedy and what wasn't there to like about that?

When she died then, in that sudden, shocking way—the mother of two young sons—it was perfectly understandable that the nation should grieve a while. On the afternoon after our wedding, a few hours after we'd heard the news, my wife and I went to a seaside resort called Whitstable for a mini-honeymoon. We sat together on the shingle beach, overhearing all the conversations—only ever about one thing—and noticing the glazed expression in everyone's eyes. It was as if a meteorite had struck. The biggest day in our lives so far—our wedding—had been completely overshadowed by history.

Not that we resented this, of course. Well you couldn't, could you, poor woman? It was only later that our doubts set in. As the days passed, the wailing and gnashing of teeth showed no signs of abating. Hundreds of thousands of mourners, the majority of whom had never known the Princess, queued up to sign the condolences book at her London home, and strew its gates with wreaths and flowers in piles as much as five feet deep. It was more than just un-British—whatever happened to the stiff upper lip?—it was actually a bit scary. For, accompanying this outbreak of mass hysteria, was a shrill, bullying imperative: "You must feel as passionately as we do. If not, then you are heartless, and evil and wrong!"

This was the period when the Queen was castigated by a tabloid newspaper—in its role as the "people's voice"—for not being seen to look sufficiently sad about her late ex-daughter-in-law's demise; when a Sardinian tourist was given a week's prison sentence for having removed a teddy bear which had been left as tribute by a mourner; when a columnist who had suggested that, perhaps, there was something a little overdone in all this mass lamentation, was upbraided by one politician: "He would have been well advised to keep his views to himself."

For well over a month, it was like living under a totalitarian state of emotional correctness. You simply didn't dare vouchsafe your inappropriate feelings to anyone but your most trusted friends. And on those rare occasions when by secret signs and elaborate circumlocution, you managed to chance upon an actual stranger who thought as you did, it was as joyous as the moment in those post-apocalypse survivor movies where the hero discovers that he is not, after all, the only human being who has not yet fallen victim to the crazy zombie virus.

Prime Minister Blair exploited all this with magisterial brilliance. At the Princess's funeral service in Westminister Abbey, he hijacked the ceremony. He read the lesson and did so with an emotional catch in his voice, the hamminess of which may have recalled Jimmy Swaggart at his most tearfully insincere, but which jelled perfectly with the national hysteria. Then in yet another typically fantastical, yet weirdly persuasive Blairite trope, he proclaimed that Diana was "the People's Princess." An extravagant claim to make about the scion of one of Britain's oldest, grandest, most aristocratic families—the Spencers. But then, being dead, Diana was in no position to quibble and Blair's appellation stuck. It was perhaps the greatest propaganda coup in his entire career. In one ingeniously chosen, perfectly timed phrase, he had managed to co-opt the most beloved woman in twentieth century British history into the modernist, populist cause of his New Labour project.

From Bastogne to Carter to Hitler to Blair to my wedding day to Princess Diana. "Sheesh!" you might be starting to worry. "I've fallen into one of those interminably digressive, art house Euro books by someone I've never heard of, like W. G. Sebald." But it's okay, you're in safe hands, I promise. It all connects to my main theme—why conservatives will always do war better than liberals—and any second now you're going to see how.

On February 15, 2003, nearly six years after Diana's funeral there was another mass display of emotional correctness in London, this time by one million marchers protesting against plans for a second Gulf War. "Not in my name," it said on their placards. "Not in my name," read their t-shirts and badges and letters to the liberal newspapers. This self-important motto prompted the caustic British columnist Julie Burchill to observe that it combined a "mixture of egotism and self-loathing that often characterizes recreational depression—an unholy alliance of Oprahism and Meldrewism in which you think you're scum but also that you're terribly important."

The British not-in-my-namers weren't alone, as journalist Nick Cohen recalled in his excoriating critique of left-liberal idiocy *What's Left?* In Ireland, the political wing of the Irish Republican Army co-ordinated the demos—terrorists for peace. In Paris, 200,000 demonstrators took to the streets; in Madrid, 650,000. In Antarctica, the American scientists at the McMurdo station came out in support. All of them—perhaps 10 million protesters around the world—opposing the overthrow of the vicious, fascist regime responsible for, among other atrocities: the brutal chemical warfare attack on the Iraqi Kurds of Halabja, killing up to 5,000 of them and injuring thousands of more; the murder of hundreds of thousands of Iraqi political dissidents; and the ruthless oppression of a nation of 24 million people.

Why were they all marching in favor of Saddam Hussein? If you'd asked any of them, they would have been appalled at the question. Of course they weren't marching *for* Saddam. They were marching *against* war. It would have struck few of them that there was any logical inconsistency in this position. By marching *against* war, they were marching in favor of a man who had done more *for* war than perhaps any other political leader in the late twentieth and early twenty-first centuries (having initiated wars against Iran, Kuwait, and his own people, and willingly accepted war with the United States and its allies not once but twice (rather than withdraw from his occupation of Kuwait and rather than abide by the terms ending the First Gulf War).

Now it wouldn't be quite true to say that the opposition to the Second Gulf war was a purely left-liberal phenomenon. Some conservatives opposed the war too, usually on the grounds of *Realpolitik*: imposing democracy by force rarely works; better the bastard you know than whatever an Islamic democracy might throw up; Iraq's tribal and religious complexities would plunge us into a quagmire of violence from which we would struggle mightily to extract ourselves; and so on. But I think we can all agree that the most vociferous and large-scale opposition came from the bleeding-heart tendency. And that what this opposition boiled down to was a simple belief that war sucks.

Or at least—let's credit them with a bit more sophistication—that war is so foully objectionable that it should never be waged except in the most extreme of circumstances. And that these circumstances weren't, in their opinion, quite extreme enough. We saw another example of this earlier on, with the 1938 Munich Agreement, remember. For Adolf Hitler read Saddam Hussein. Saddam knew, as Hitler knew, that liberal squeamishness within Western democracy is a dictator's best friend.

Lenin knew this too, when he came up with his most celebrated maxim: "Probe with a bayonet: if you meet steel, stop. If you meet mush, push." Revolutionaries and rogue states the world over have been enthusiastically following his advice ever since: from Che Guevera and Fidel Castro to the Iraqi insurgency to the Iranian revolutionary government to North Korea. They follow it because almost unfailingly, it works. It's the first principle of asymmetric warfare.

But was Lenin's maxim really so clever? Any child of eight could tell you exactly the same thing. As a kid, you know that while your parents hold all the power—the money, the bedtime and screen-time control, the right of veto—it's still quite stupidly easy to get your way. All you have to do is nag and nag and nag and *nag* and eventually your parents will cave in. You know they'll cave in because they almost always do. It has to be some really major issue before they won't cave in and when that issue arises, well, obviously you throw a huge tantrum to show how much your parents are going to suffer if ever they thwart you like this again. Secretly though, you're thinking: "Wow. They finally stood up to me. Wonder why they don't do it more?"

Now that I'm a parent, I know full well why parents are so useless at disciplining their children. Partly it's an ignorance thing. At any stage of their development, children are always way more advanced than their parents—in their fond "Ah, she's still just my little baby," infantilising way—imagine they are. Consequently, your kids will always run intellectual rings around you and lie and cheat and trick more fluently than ever you dreamed possible of such darling, perfect innocents.

Partly, too, it's the love thing. You adore your children so much you will try to avoid anything that causes them distress of any kind. Making them do anything they don't want to do, say.

Does any of this have any bearing on the relationship between democratic Western superpowers and their sundry rogue-state and terrorist rivals? You bet it does. One of the great mistakes we make with our enemies, as we do with our children, is to underestimate their sophistication and guile. We think because they come from two-bit hell-holes where diarrhea is a way of life that they haven't read all the clever books we have, boned up on our theories, our social structures and worked out how best to exploit them.

Our fetishization of "Human Rights," for example. You think it's an accident that the global Islamist movement has managed to make so much political capital out of Abu Ghraib and Guantanamo? Then consider the al Qaeda training manual found in Manchester in 2003. Its Rule 18 ordered that their terrorists, if captured, "must insist on proving that torture was inflicted on them" and "complain to the court of mistreatment while in prison." As British writer Douglas Murray comments in his rous-ing *Neoconservatism: Why We Need It* (Social Affairs Unit): "We are allowing the advances that our society has fought for to be used against us, and used to drag us into darkness."

Perhaps the second half of the parent/child analogy—the one to do with love—isn't quite so obviously apposite. But think of that love, instead, in terms of "liberal guilt"—and suddenly that too makes perfect sense. By the mere fact of our global hegemony, this strain of thinking goes, we have done wrong to lesser states and must therefore make amends by acceding whenever possible to their demands.

This emotional approach, however, is as counterproductive in foreign policy matters as it is in childrearing ones. When you're about to go on a long family walk and your child screams that he doesn't want to go, it's boring, he's tired, his leg hurts, your imme-diate temptation might be to give in. After all, it's not going to kill him if he doesn't go, the walk will be much more pleasant for the rest of you if Grumbler stays behind watching TV, and it's hardly one of those make-or-break issues that you feel like fighting a huge battle over.

Those are some of the excuses you'll make for yourself, as you think about caving in. But if you do cave in, you're not just a wuss and fool but you've betrayed your whole family. You've taught Grumbler that tantrums work. You've denied him the exercise that would have made him healthier and happier, and you've denied him the opportunity of gradually discovering that walks are in fact one of life's greatest pleasures. You've also made a dividing line within the family, creating schism and rivalry (what's Grumbler's sister going to think about this arrangement?) where there should be companionship and shared goals.

Foreign policy's really no different. All your emotions may tell you that playing hardball with less powerful states isn't nice: it makes you feel like a big bully and it makes them unhappy. Just listen to them, telling you how unhappy it makes them. They say you're a great Satan, an imperialist aggressor, that you're only in this for the oil, that you're racist, that you hate their religion, that you won't be happy till you've conquered all the world, that you're not a liberator but an occupier, that you're starving their children, that you're horrid, and mean, and cruel. Shame on you, Great Satan! If you want to stand a hope of redeeming yourself, there's only one thing you can do: slink back to your infernal den and leave our earthly paradise well alone.

It's at times like these that you need to behave like a grown-up. You need to think beyond the visceral and the immediate—the realm of childhood—and consider the bigger picture. War may be bad, intervention may be a form of bullying, but what if these are the least worst options? What if maybe in the longer term you're doing these countries a favor by easing them on the path from dictatorship towards democracy? What about all those voices in those countries we never get to hear because they're always being drowned out by the screaming, professional Great-Satan-and-Little-Satan-haters? What about the homosexuals, the women, the guys who want to make a living selling pop CDs, DVDs, or even beer without having their stores smashed or their heads chopped off? What about the folks back home who will be able sleep a little more safely in their beds, knowing that thanks to vigorous Coalition intervention the global terror movement is being denied secure foreign strongholds and training grounds? What about the fact that, living as we do in a global economy where issues like the security of the oil supply are of massive concern to everyone, a policy of non-interventionism is in any case naïve to the point of suicide?

In older, better times, the leaders of the free world understood this. "Enlightened self-interest" was the watchword of all sensible foreign policy makers. If you believe, as they unashamedly did, that the values of your nation are values which the rest of the globe should be proud to share, then whenever your country acts in its own interests it will be doing the whole world a favor.

Anti-imperialists tend to get terribly worked up about details like Imperial Britain's "gunboat diplomacy" policy in the late nineteenth century, whereby any smaller power that didn't do as Britain wished would swiftly be obliged to change its mind with a few shots from a Royal Navy warship. This was, for example, how Britain for many years went on preserving her inalienable right to go on profiting from the Chinese opium trade and keeping a whole nation enslaved by addiction.

But just because great powers are capable of doing bad things and making mistakes hardly constitutes an argument that they should butt out of international intervention, period. Many years ago, in a market in El Fasher in the Western Sudan, I was accosted by an elderly Sudanese gentleman. "Why did you leave us?" he said on discovering I was British. "Our country was so much better when you were running it." Given the Islamist terror state Sudan has become since, my friend may have had a point. And El Fasher, of course, is one of the main towns in Darfur—the province where hundreds of thousands of Christian and Animist men, women, and children have been massacred as a form of ethnic cleansing by a government-backed militia called the Janjaweed.

Between the moral certainty and self-belief our nations shared until at least the end of the Second World War, and the self-doubt and moral relativism that afflicts us now, I'm in no doubt which is preferable. As I write, there are tales in our press about a British human rights lawyer who has taken up the case of two alleged Iraqi war criminals. The story is what's known in the trade as a marmalade-dropper: one so truly shocking that it throws your breakfast into a state of chaos.

Here are the details: in March 2003 two British soldiers, Staff Sergeant Simon Cullingworth and Sapper Luke Allsopp, were travelling in a convoy that was ambushed by Fedayeen militiamen on the outskirts of Al Zubayr in southern Iraq. They were seized and badly beaten. Then, wounded and in terrible pain, they were driven to an Iraqi intelligence base. There they were murdered in cold blood, gunned down while a baying mob of grinning Iraqis took trophy pictures.

Once the alleged killers had been captured, the British Royal Military Police—following the rule of law to the letter—submitted a file of evidence to the Central Criminal Court of Iraq, which in turn passed the case on to the Iraq Higher Tribunal. Now, however, in an application which is being funded through "legal aid" paid for by the British taxpayer, a British lawyer is arguing that the Iraq Higher Tribunal is a "politicised court" which might jeopardize alleged killers' human rights under Article 3 of the European Convention of Human Rights. Therefore they should be tried in Britain, where they will be sentenced more leniently.

No halfway sane person could read that story without choking on their cornflakes. The stupidity and injustice of it are so utterly manifest as to brook no reasonable argument. "And what about the Human Rights of the poor guys who were murdered?" you want to scream. "And since when was it a British lawyer's job to fight for the rights of Iraqis charged with committing Iraq-based crimes NOT to be tried by an Iraq-based court?" "How much is he being paid for this?" "What kind of warped motivation leads him to imagine that there's any kind of justice in this?" "Why am I paying his bills?" "What kind of message is this going to send out to future killers-in-cold-blood of British prisoners?"

It's one of those cases, in fact, that could have been dreamed up by a conservative expressly to illustrate everything that's wrong with the Left-liberal position on pretty much everything. In one, devastating blow, it puts paid to all remaining doubts about the fundamental idiocy and malignity of: moral and cultural relativism, "human rights" legislation, the European Union, human rights lawyers, multiculturalism, the United Nations.... (I'm not sure the United Nations was necessarily involved here, but I'm with John Bolton on this one: "The Secretariat building in New York has thirty-eight stories. If it lost ten stories it wouldn't make a difference." Except I say: "Why stop at ten?")

So if remorseless logic is so obviously on their side, how come conservatives still so often lose the debate? How come, for example, the thing that undid Tony Blair was not his disastrous Socialism-Lite domestic policy but his principled stance on the war on terror? How come George W. Bush has been so successfully caricatured as a dumb warmonger? How come, even after the Surge, the popular verdict on Iraq is that of Vietnam-revisited? How come so few European nations are pulling their weight in Afghanistan?

The answer, funnily enough, lies in that first question. Having all the arguments on your side can often be a weakness, not a strength, because it makes you complacent and arrogant. Consider Donald Rumsfeld's memorable Iraq war briefings. I loved them and I expect you did too, for their confidence, their no-bullshit swagger, the way they cheerfully drove a coach and horses through all that cautious, evasive, mealy-mouthed, corporate-speak we've come to expect from public figures these days. I also loved them for the way they set my anti-war friends' teeth on edge. The peaceniks may not have wanted to overthrow Saddam. But, by golly, they could happily have murdered Rummy.

Problem is, I don't think Rummy's preening self-possession did the conservative cause many favors. I don't think Dubya's joshing, frat boy ease did so either. They spoke to conservatives well enough, but conservatives weren't really the people who needed convincing. The broader culture, let's not forget, speaks the language of the liberal-left. Unless you can engage it in those terms, you're never going to swing it round to your point of view.

That language is, of course, not the language of logic, reason, and commonsense but the language of emotion. This was the language a worryingly large part of Britain was speaking after the death of Diana. The language Tony Blair exploited when he led New Labour into power. And very unfortunately for you, the language most of America is speaking—and will continue to speak for many years—in the wake of President Obama's election.

Among Blair's much-trumpeted innovations when he swept into power was his new Ethical Foreign Policy. Did this mean ending arms sales to the governments of impoverished countries which could ill afford them? Not quite: that might have jeopardized the lucrative 28 million pound air defense system it sold to Tanzania. Did it perhaps mean an end to bribes? Nope: in 2008, Blair quietly halted an official anti-bribery investigation when it emerged that this might affect a 20 billion pound Saudi arms deal.

But in the earlier part of his tenure, he did at least get a couple of opportunities to demonstrate sort of what he meant when two lovely, good wars were dropped into his lap. Liberal-lefties do love a good war. It's their chance to show to the world that they're not the craven, lily-livered, panty-waist, tofu-munching surrender monkeys the conservatives claim they are. That in fact, when push comes to shove, they can be as tough and fierce as any gun-toting, right-wing baby-muncher.

Problem with good wars is they're so very hard to find. The Second World War, some say, was the last truly noble cause—but even that one was pretty murky, when you think of the moral compromises that had to be made by cosying up to mass-murderer Stalin. Then there's the wrinkle that if a war is to count as a war it is almost certain to involve people getting killed. And that's not nice. At the very least it will involve the deaths of your enemies who, enemies though they may be, are very likely to come from countries poorer than yours, ergo qualifying them as oppressed victims more deserving of sympathy than destruction. At worst, it means bringing your boys and (increasingly, in these times of state-enforced equal opportunities) girls home in body bags, which never plays well with any electorate but particularly not a left-liberal voting one. They voted you in because you were supposed to be against this kind of thing, right?

Hence Blair's undisguised glee at the chance to intervene in the former Yugoslav state of Kosovo in 1999 and in the vicious civil war in the West African country of Sierra Leone (formerly a British colony) in 2000. Short duration; minimal body-count; relatively low cost; generally positive outcome. If only all wars could be this way.

But as history could have told Tony Blair, if only he hadn't been so busy trying to abolish it, wars generally don't work out that way because war is by nature a messy, bloody, protracted business. Even in asymmetrical modern warfare—where you have total air superiority, Abrams tanks and cruise missiles, and about the heaviest thing the enemy has to chuck back at you is mortar rounds, IEDs, and RPGs—even then, you can win all the set piece battles and still lose the war if you're not prepared to put boots on the ground to secure the peace.

This means spending money on the armed forces. Lots more money than most Democrats would ever countenance, especially if their name is Barney Frank of Massachusetts. Also lots more money—let's be honest here—than many conservatives have been prepared to vouchsafe in recent years. It was under Bush Senior, after all, that the United States first took advantage of the supposed "peace dividend" by downsizing its military, pushing officers into early retirement, and mothballing ships. (Though of course, it got much worse under Clinton.) It was under conservative Prime Minister Margaret Thatcher that the Options for Change defense cuts were introduced, whereby the British military lost 18 percent of its manpower and a good many of the regiments which had helped win World Wars One and Two.

The people who have benefited least from the "peace dividend" are, of course, the very ones we should be supporting most: our boys and girls in the military. We are asking them to achieve more and more—Iraq, Afghanistan, then where?—with less and less manpower. And in Britain's case, certainly, with outmoded equipment that just isn't up to the job. So far, more than thirty British soldiers have been killed by mines and IEDs in Iraq and Afghanistan as a direct result of our Government's failure to provide them with properly armored vehicles, rather than the thin-skinned Snatch Land Rovers designed for use in Northern Ireland.

Yes, we'll concede that even our conservative politicians have not loved our military quite as much as they ought, these last two decades. But let us never be in any doubt that the mindset responsible for the parlous state of our armed forces is essentially a left-liberal one. It is the liberal-left, after all, which holds as one of its dearest articles of faith that human nature is capable of improvement. If this is so, then warfare is something man will engage in less and less as—tutored, no doubt, by the beneficent state—he learns to control his violent impulses, and solve all the world's ills through peaceful negotiation.

Conservatives have no truck with such idealistic tosh. They've studied their history and they fully agree with Plato on this one: "Only the dead have seen the end of war." Man, they understand, is intrinsically, atavistically, and incorrigibly a creature of violence. No amount of cultural enlightenment is going to alter this. Prolonged exposure to Schubert did not stop the Nazis killing six million Jews. Acid house and Ecstasy culture did not prevent Srebrenica. The nation that fails to prepare itself sufficiently for war, therefore, is the nation that is asking to get itself squashed.

Sure there will always be the odd lucky exception to this rule. Like wartime Switzerland: too geographically complicated to be worth invading. Like modern Germany: happy to let Britain and the United States do most of its fighting for it in the war on terror because, hey what are they going to do about it, nuke Berlin? But just because some countries get to opt out doesn't alter this ineluctable truth: if you feel your culture is worth defending then you need to keep all options open, up to and including the ability to fight a bloody, full scale war.

You don't want to fight this war, of course. No one in their right mind does. It's not the conservative position that war is a fun thing or a desirable thing. Merely that it's sometimes a necessary thing and that if you're going to fight it, you don't want to do it with one arm tied behind your back. You want to do it quickly, with all your might, and you want to make damn sure that you win. Otherwise what's the point?

Those of us who grew up in the shadow of the Soviet nuclear threat will remember the constant, low-level nagging anxiety which came from never being quite sure whether or not today was going to be the day when you were vaporized. It's a relief that the Cold War is over but I'm not altogether convinced that the aftermath is a great improvement. Islamist terrorists have already killed many more people on the British and United States home fronts than the Russians or the Chinese ever did. And I can't say I've noticed any massive diminution in the number of wars we need to fight to preserve our interests. The main difference seems to be that we've decided we can now afford to spend less on our defense.

Does this fill you with confidence? It doesn't me. I don't particularly want to die at the hands of a crazed Islamist. I don't want my children to die in the grips of one. I don't want you to die that way either. And it seems to me the best way to prevent that is to take the Islamist threat seriously, increase the size of our militaries, and root out and kill the terrorists before they kill us. But there seem to be an awful lot of people out there who want to believe that if only we talk to the terrorists and our international enemies, they'll suddenly become our bestest, bosomest buddies, especially once they see nice Mr. Obama in the White House. (But don't we in any case talk to our enemies through "back channels" all the time; the answer is: of course we do—but we know how little reality impinges on left-liberal positions.)

Adolf Hitler never made any great secret of what he planned to do to the world. Nor did the Soviets ("We will bury you.") Nor do the Islamists.

"We are not fighting so that you will offer us something" says Hussein Mussawi, former leader of Hezbollah. "We are fighting you to eliminate you."

Samuel Huntington nailed the problem in his *The Clash of Civilizations and the Remaking of World Order*. "The West won the world not by the superiority of its ideas or values or religion, but rather by its superiority in applying organized violence. Westerners often forget this fact, non-Westerners never do."

Conclusion

WHAT REALLY MATTERS

WELL, WE'RE NEARLY DONE and I know just how you're feeling.

Terrible.

The land you love has been hijacked by a bunch of left-liberal fruitcakes. They don't have much of an idea how to fix the economy. But they do know exactly how to ruin your life. And they will.

Over the next long, weary years, your taxes are going to rise, your standard of living is going to drop, and—maybe the worst thing of all for free Americans—your liberties are going to be curtailed.

Socialists don't believe in freedom. And socialism is what you've now got. Maybe they won't call it that, but the results will be the same. They'll dress it up with nice-sounding phrases like "equality," "fairness," "social justice," "freedom of choice," "environmental care," "affirmative action," "multiculturalism," "carbon emissions reduction," "negotiated settlement," "ethical foreign policy," "animal rights," and "consumer protection." But you personally won't feel the remotest benefit from this. All you'll notice is that you've less money to spend, that there seem to be more and more restrictions on what you're allowed to do, and that you have less and less influence over the remote, faceless apparatchiks now controlling your existence.

Socialists distrust individuals. That's why your future will be less about what's good for you and more and more about what's good for the country. Not what you think is good for the country—*your* thinking is now officially incorrect—but what Big Government has decided in its wisdom is good for the country. Big Brother makes the rules from now on. Nanny knows what's best.

You may not like what Nanny says, because Nanny now seems determined to stray into areas where you thought Nanny had no place: gun ownership; your freedom to hunt; how you dispose of your tax; where your church is permitted to stand on abortion; how you bring up your kids.

But if you don't like this, tough. Because socialism distrusts individuals, it will always seek to transfer sovereignty upwards—away from you and towards a remote, less democratically accountable higher authority. No longer can you make your own decisions. Increasingly, not even your local or state government will be able to reflect your needs and preferences. When Big Government takes charge, it really means Big Government. In Britain, now, 80 percent of all new laws emanate not from our elected parliamentarians, but from the unelected, uncontrollable mandarins who run the European Socialist Superstate (aka the EU). You read that right: 80 percent of all new laws in Britain are laws over which the people have had no say whatsoever.

This is the socialist way. This is how it will now be in America, with federal judges—politically correct appointees of the Democrat administration, of course—making rules which your local representatives have no right to veto. Nanny knows best, remember.

I'm sorry; now I've summed it all up so bluntly—without any of those weird digressions or silly asides to sweeten the pill—you're probably feeling more depressed than ever.

In fact you might even be feeling, as I often do, a bit like that scene in *Platoon*. Your firebase has been overrun, your defense has collapsed, Charlie's swarming all over your trenches and killing all your buddies. All you can do now is retreat to your bunker, call down your artillery on your own position, and rejoice in the sheer bloody hell of your utter destruction. The catharsis of *Götterdämmerung*.

Trust me, though, it's not as bad as you think. Actually, no, it is as bad as you think but that's really no reason for killing yourself.

Consolation number one. It could be worse. You could be living in Britain. We've had well over a decade of this nightmare already, remember, with a lot more bad stuff still to come because the socialists are still in charge. We're presided over by an even more socialistically inclined regime in Europe, and with an economy officially in worse shape than any country's you've heard of save, maybe, Pakistan's.

Consolation number two. It can't last forever. Nothing ever does. When the Obama project has failed—more important, when it has been seen to fail by an utterly disillusioned electorate—you get to crow "I told you so" and will finally get invited to all the best parties as the prophet who knew it all along.

Consolation number three. You know you're right. And I hope, having read this book, you'll have an even better idea why you're right. This is important. All too often we conservatives are lazily caricatured as the evil ones, the selfish ones, and after a time it wears you down. You might even start wondering, in your more vulnerable moments, whether maybe your left-liberal opponents have a point.

Nil Illegitimi Carborundum—as we'd all still be saying if our education systems hadn't been so debased by the progressives.

Don't let the bastards grind you down, because they have no moral cause to do so. You have all the arguments. Not them.

But I do know how hard it can be sometimes. Like, the other night, at dinner, I found myself arguing with a woman who thought my views on our state-run National Health Service were heartless and selfish and bad. "Suppose you were too poor to afford health insurance and you had a child sick with leukaemia. Are you saying it's okay for that kid to be allowed to just... die?"

This is what I call the cute kitten argument: "If you vote Republican this cute wounded little kitten with the bandaged paw will die." Whereas, presumably, if you vote Democrat, this kitten will make a full recovery and breed lots of even cuter kittens so that one day there'll be a cute kitten in every household and the world will live happily ever after.

When the cute kitten argument is invoked it's all too easy—because it's such a mean, low-down, typically left-liberal ploy—to be riled and go too far the other way. You start playing up to the popular image people have of conservatives. "Yes, yes!" you go. "If it's a question of my liberty, my taxes, well I'd kill not just that cute wounded kitten, but the whole of the darned cat kingdom if I had to. I'd kill those clever cats from Lake Van in Turkey that can swim. And the sweet ones in the calendars with different colored eyes, like David Bowie has. And the Siamese cats, and the Burmese cats, and the Tonkinese cats, and the Thomas O'Malley Alley cats. And Top Cat. And the cast of Andrew Lloyd-Webber's *Cats*. And the spotted endangered jungle species cats. And the Big Cats. And the little cats. And especially the baby cats. It's those kittens that I want to kill most of all because that's the kind of guy I am. I'm a conservative.'

This is a mistake. You know as soon as you've said it it's a mistake. And you know it's still more of a mistake once you've played it over again in your head, in the sober light of day.

It's a mistake because have you played right into the hands of the enemy, falling into their elephant trap, confirming all their worst suspicions about what it is that conservatives stand for. And it's a mistake because it's not even true. You don't believe in killing cute wounded kittens with bandaged paws. You don't want the poor kid with leukaemia to die. There are no more conservatives who think that way than there are left-liberals who think that way. This kitten, this imaginary poor kid with leukaemia—they're just red herrings; straw men.

That's why, when the sick kitten elephant trap is placed in front of you, it's very important NOT to step crossly straight into it. What you need to do instead is to take a deep breath—a very deep breath—and get back to first principles.

"I am not a conservative because I am evil and selfish and wrong," you need to remind yourself. "I am a conservative because in a flawed world where nothing can ever be truly fair, my philosophy is the least worst way of creating social justice and abundance for all."

Take taxes. (*PLEASE!*) The reason you believe in low taxes is not just because you're selfish. (If, that is, you buy the line that selfishness is a wholly bad thing, which if you read Adam Smith, you realize isn't the case anyway.) It's because the more money free individuals have available to spend, the faster the economy will grow, benefiting everyone—rich and poor alike. It's also because you believe taxation is just a form of legitimized theft. Since when did faceless bureaucrats and two-bit careerist politicos know better how to spend your hard-earned money than you do? Since when did governments get this irresponsible idea that the vast budgets they spend every year belong to them? They don't. That money is your money.

So, to get back to the imaginary child with leukaemia, of course you don't want him to die. What you want is an economy so successful and abundant that even the poorest can afford the necessary health insurance. But you don't create an economy like that through higher taxes and greater government spending. Quite the opposite. That's why you're a conservative.

And you're also conservative because you believe in conserving things. This means you instinctively care for all that is good and beautiful in the natural world. You don't need some hair shirt, yogurt-weaving green with hair like Sideshow Bob or, worse, some jet-setting, multiple-mansion-maintaining, failed presidential candidate lecturing you on your environmental responsibilities. You already know. It's in the blood. It's why you like the outdoors and wholesome, natural pursuits like hunting and fishing. And why you instinctively distrust all this apocalyptic talk of climate change (hasn't climate been changing for, like, millennia?) and of solutions so radical they'll do more damage than the problems they're supposedly going to solve. Wind farms are a good example of this. Their power generation capacity is minimal, erratic, and only economically viable with heavy taxpayer subsidy. Yet purely because some eco-fascist ideologue decided sometime that they're good, these noisy, bird-chewing monsters are now being allowed to despoil our pristine, beautiful landscapes in the name of *conservation*.

As a conservative you believe in tradition. You like tradition not just because it's quirky, handcrafted, has the attractive patina of age, tells a great story, and is probably quite valuable, but also because tradition is something that has evolved through time and lasted through time, and has therefore been assessed by generation after generation as something worth keeping. Why should your generation be so arrogant as to think it knows better? You believe that if it ain't broke, it doesn't need fixing. And you're suspicious of dazzling new theories which seek to overturn tradition, because they're just theories. Theories are a dime a dozen and

there's a new one every ten minutes. Tradition is the work of centuries.

As a conservative you believe in liberty. Liberty means that so
long as you harm no others and unless there's a damn good reason otherwise—conscription in time of war, maybe: but it had better be a pretty major war. Bigger than Nam, I'd say—you should
be free to live your life exactly as you please. The government has
no business in your private life. Only you know what's good for
you. And I include in that even stuff that's bad for you like cigarettes. If you want to die of lung cancer that is your choice. And
don't give me that nonsense about passive smoking. Passive smoking is a myth—as the only ever serious long term, large scale
research program into the subject (by James Enstrom and Geof-
frey Kabat) demonstrated. The only reason we believe otherwise
is that—just as they did with AIDS—our governments believe that
if they told us the truth we would reach the wrong decision.
Therefore they lie. It's for our own good, don't you know?

As a conservative you believe in equality. But most definitely
not as President Obama and his friends would understand it. Your
version of equality is not about rigging the system in the name of
"fairness" so that certain favored minorities feel better about
themselves. It's about making sure everyone, so far as is reasonably possible, gets an even break. And above all that everyone is
equal in the eyes of the law.

As a conservative you believe in your country: what it stands
for (liberty), how it got to what it stands for (hard work, courage,
and sacrifice), and its core values (God, King, and Country, in the
English formulation; faith, family, and freedom in the American;
both within the tradition of Western, Greco-Roman, Judaeo-
Christian, Anglo-Saxon civilization). You respect those core values, and you will, if necessary, fight to the death to defend those
core values. You do not believe all cultures are equal. If you did,

why not just swap places with someone in one of those countries where girls who have been mass-raped are stoned to death for adultery or which practice female circumcision?

As a conservative you believe in proper, old-fashioned teaching methods that really work; you believe in rigor—not dumbing down; you believe in times-tables for math, dates for history, grammar for English; you believe in Latin (even if your own knowledge of it is either shaky or non-existent); you believe a healthy mind in a sound body, *mens sana in corpore sano*; you believe in sports for kids even if you were no good at them yourself; you believe that competition is a healthy thing; that elitism is not a dirty word. You believe in standards.

You believe in all these things—and in many other worthwhile causes too numerous to mention—because, unlike left-liberals, you are not racked with self-loathing. You don't necessarily believe in some barmy, Rousseau-esque way that all human beings are innately good. ("Neither conservatives nor humorists believe man is good. But left-wingers do"—P. J. O'Rourke.) But what you do believe is that free individuals, left more or less to their own devices, will behave in such a way as leads ultimately to the greater benefit of all mankind. And that when government tries to trammel human behavior in the name of social justice, it invariably makes things worse, not better.

And just because you believe all this does not make you a bad person. Nor does it mean—as your liberal-left enemies would sometimes seek to imply—that you are bad in bed, that you have no fashion sense, that you have poor taste in music, or that you are not cool. On all these points remember that Ian Fleming, a Tory, created James Bond as a conservative. All the heroic virtues, after all, are conservative ones.

Feel better now? You should. Say it loud and proud: "I'm a conservative."

Consolation number four. Personally, I think that this one is the most important consolation you can possibly draw from this book. But then I would, for reasons which will soon become obvious. You know how much better it is to give than to receive? You know what a wonderful warm glow you get when you help the deserving poor? Well there's a guy I know—you'd like him I think: quite funny, family guy, believes in all the things you believe in, apart from maybe drugs (he's maybe a bit too liberal on drugs)— and he's been living for far too long under an oppressive, high-taxing, socialist nanny state with a collapsing economy which makes your political situation look like the golden years of Reagan.

This guy—let's call him James: that is, after all, his name—is in trouble. But with a little help from you he can get out of that trouble. You, yes YOU, dear right-thinking reader have the power to transform his life.

Here's how. Each copy of this book sold means that James's life just gets better and better.

1 copy sold buys, well, not much really but at least spares him the humiliation of having sold no copies whatsoever.

10 copies buys him a decent cigar to wave ostentatiously in the faces of the anti-smoking police.

100 copies pays the "cap" for a day's foxhunting. The illegal kind of foxhunting preferably where—"Oops! We seem accidentally to have bagged an actual fox..."

1,000 copies pays for maybe a week's schooling for Boy. Yeah—I told you it was expensive. Imagine how much more if he hadn't got his 40 percent scholarship.

10,000 copies pays for maybe quarter of a year's interest-only mortgage repayment on the family house now rendered almost worthless, thanks in good part to my socialist government's reckless overspending on unsustainable welfare programs and expanding the number of people doing non-jobs in State employment.

100,000 copies starts to make James think that maybe his life has not, after all, been a total waste of time. That there is a divine justice at work in the world. Now he can afford a car to replace his battered Ford Mondeo. Maybe a powerful 4 x 4 SUV to wind-up his electric-car-driving eco friends down the road. A Range Rover Sport? God, he loves that car. So do his kids. Especially the screens in the back, on which you can watch *South Park* DVDs while Dad's trying to point out boring grown-up stuff like ruined monasteries. "Hey kids. Look outside. There's Tintern Abbey." "Huh huh huh huh. A rat just ate Kenny's face off."

1,000,000 copies spells joy unconfined. James's wife has been promised that if this book enjoys any kind of major commercial success, she will be allowed: new boots from Emma Hope; a new coat from Marni; new jewellery; new, whatever. When the wife's happy, you're happy. Ain't that true, guys?

2,000,000 copies and James loves you, America. Now he can fulfill his lifelong dream of retiring to the country, buying a small estate, and spending his days riding to hounds, shooting pheasant, and maybe writing the odd World War II adventure novel, just to keep his hand in. Either that or he can spend every last penny of it on Boy's education. And in the unlikely event there's anything left, on darling Girl's too.

5,000,000 copies. Does this ever happen? Possibly not. But if it does, James's gratitude will be so great that he promises forthwith to become an American citizen, perhaps as a springboard to becoming your president (you might need to amend your Constitution to let him do this, but it would be worth it). Once installed in the White House, he promises to: lower taxes; dismantle ex-president Obama's disastrous welfare programs; appoint Rush Limbaugh editor of the *New York Times* and Ann Coulter editor of *Vanity Fair*; put Mark Steyn in charge of foreign policy; break off all diplomatic relations with socialist old Europe, but forge stronger ties with countries that "get" the war on terror, like

Poland; bring the UK into NAFTA, in preparation for its eventual admission as America's 51st state; create eternal peace, abundance, and happiness for all mankind.

Now you know what to do. Thanks for listening.

ACKNOWLEDGMENTS

THIS BOOK WOULD NOT EXIST without the brilliance of Harry Crocker III, vice president and executive editor of Regnery books, who appeared suddenly and unexpectedly in my life, said "Fiat" and made it so. Thank you, Harry. You are a hero. Thanks also to the rest of the brilliant team at Regnery. You have made me love the American way EVEN MORE than I did before, if that's possible.

Thanks to my agent Peter Straus of Rogers, Coleridge and White for reminding me that though U.S. deals are nice, a guy still needs to feed his family.

Thanks to my wife for feeding me, humoring me, and generally putting up with me during the writing process.

Thanks to my Uncle Perce for use of his Devon flat for the family holiday which was completely ruined by my suddenly having to write a book.

Thanks to my father for saying encouraging things when I sent him sample chapters.

Thanks to my sister for chanting for me.

Thanks to Paul McKenna for helping brainwash me (in a nice way) to get it done.

Thanks to Barack Obama for getting elected—because if he hadn't been this book would have been in deep trouble.

Thanks to W, my best American friend for the long, impassioned email he sent trying to warn me off writing it.

Thanks to P. J. O'Rourke's *Republican Party Reptile* for setting me on the path of righteousness, and to Mark Steyn's *America Alone* for keeping me on it.

Thanks to all those friends, acquaintances, and role models, who helped and advised me on the way, and especially to the writers whose ingenious tropes and erudite references I may shamelessly have filched during the writing of this book. I have tried wherever possible to acknowledge my sources in the text. If I haven't, this is pure oversight rather than a deliberate and sinister attempt to pass off as my own the ideas of my betters.

They include, in no particular order, Douglas Murray; Johnny Foreman; Harry Mount; Damian Thompson; Andrew Roberts; David Pryce Jones; Stuart Reid; Tom Burkard (whose *Inside The Secret Garden*—University of Buckingham Press—came in very handy for the Education chapter); Pat Michaels (whose *Meltdown* (Cato) was useful for the polar bear chapter); St. Christopher Booker; Professor Philip Stott; Rod Liddle; Stephen Daneff; Daniel Hannan MEP; Brendan O'Neill; Roger and Sophie Scruton; Anthony Browne; David Craig; David S Taylor; Peter Whittle; Jessica Douglas-Home; David Conway; Michael Gove MP; Patrick West (author of *Conspicuous Compassion*); Nick Cohen; Robert Hardman; Toby Young; Matt D'Ancona; John Hart; Civitas; the Social Affairs Unit; Spiked; The Institute of Ideas; Trey Parker and

Matt Stone; Freddy Gray; Tania and Jamie Compton; all those other nice people who, inexcusably, I have forgotten to include.

Thanks finally to Tony Blair, Gordon Brown, Ken Livingstone, John Prescott, Al Gore, Michael Moore, Noam Chomsky, and left-liberal politicians, "thinkers," apparatchiks, fellow travellers, and hangers-on everywhere for helping to fill me with the disgust and bile which made this book such a pleasure and a relief to write.

INDEX